THE REVISED DEFINITIVE
EDITIONS OF THE WORKS
OF WILLIAM GERHARDIE

ANTON CHEHOV

The Works of William Gerhardie:

Novels

FUTILITY: *A Novel on Russian Themes*
THE POLYGLOTS
DOOM
PENDING HEAVEN
THE MEMOIRS OF SATAN (*with Brian Lunn*)
RESURRECTION
OF MORTAL LOVE
MY WIFE'S THE LEAST OF IT

Short Novels: collected

PRETTY CREATURES

Drama

DONNA QUIXOTE: *A Lyrical Comedy*
I WAS A KING IN BABYLON – AND YOU MAY VERY WELL BE RIGHT: *An Implausible Comedy*
RASPUTIN: *The Ironical Tragedy*

Cristicism and Biography

ANTON CHEHOV: *A Critical Study*
MY LITERARY CREDO

Autobiography

MEMOIRS OF A POLYGLOT

Biographical History

THE ROMANOFFS

Collaborations
with Hugh Kingsmill

THE CASANOVA FABLE:
THE SUMMING UP

with Prince Leopold of Loewenstein

MEET YOURSELF:
studies in self-analysis

ANTON CHEHOV

A Critical Study

PREFACE BY
MICHAEL HOLROYD

ST. MARTIN'S PRESS
NEW YORK

 For information, write:
St. Martin's Press, Inc., 175 Fifth Ave., New York, N.Y. 10010
Printed in Great Britain
Library of Congress Catalog Card Number: 73-93997
First published in the United States of America in 1975

CONTENTS

PREFACE BY MICHAEL HOLROYD

CHAPTER PAGE

I. THE EFFECT OF HIS WORK, ITS PECULIAR UNIQUENESS 7

II. THE SENSIBILITY WHICH NECESSITATED THIS EXPRESSION 22

III. THE DETERMINING CAUSES OF HIS SENSIBILITY; AND THE RELEVANT CIRCUMSTANCES OF HIS LIFE . . . 45

IV. THE MEANS BY WHICH HIS SENSIBILITY WAS GIVEN EXPRESSION: A TECHNICAL EXAMINATION OF HIS STYLE . . . 78

V. A CLOSER EXAMINATION OF PERFECTLY CHARACTERISTIC PASSAGES IN WHICH HIS SENSIBILITY IS COMPLETELY EXPRESSED . 123

AUTHOR'S EPILOGUE 155

MY LITERARY CREDO 157

PREFACE

MICHAEL HOLROYD

'There is a book,' wrote Desmond MacCarthy in the *New Statesman*, 'no one interested in Chekhov's work should miss reading. It has been out some time, and it is by Mr William Gerhardie who wrote that admirable novel about Russian life, *Futility*. This critical study is one of the best I have read. I do not feel that it is too late to recommend this book, because it is one that will find a permanent place in any library of critical literature.'

Written, for the most part, while Gerhardie was up at Oxford, *Anton Chehov* was published in 1923, a year after *Futility* had appeared. It was the first critical study of Chehov in any language, not excluding Russian. In America, where its publication coincided with the appearance of the Moscow Art Theatre, it met, as in England, with general acclaim, the *New York Times* in a mammoth review hailing it as 'one of the ablest critical studies of recent years,' and adding: 'It is certainly the most delightful.' To-day, in Soviet Russia, it is spoken of as a standard work; while to English readers it has remained one of the most authoritative studies available.

Gerhardie was uniquely placed to write this book. As both *Futility* and *The Polyglots*, his next novel on Russian themes, show, his own writing, though it sparkles with more comic absurdity, is deeply influenced by Chehov. Born in old St Petersburg of English parents, Gerhardie had attended a preparatory and two secondary Russian schools before going to Oxford and had been brought up bilingual.

By the 1920s certain British critics, such as Middleton Murry, had, without owning a word of Russian, made a corner for themselves in the Constance Garnett translations. Murry, in fact, reviewed this book at length in the *Times Literary Supplement* in a manner suggesting that the author was in a stage of development from which he, Murry, had just emerged, and that he was watching Gerhardie's progress with hope from a point further along the road. But Gerhardie had already sailed up wind of his reviewer by demonstrating that the humour and lyricism which suffuse Chehov's original have a trick of evaporating in translation and that the Garnett rendering was essentially an approximation, echoing a certain melodious tone at some expense of good English, and letting the humour go. It was thus that Gerhardie became, in the words of C. P. Snow, 'the first person in England actively to interpret Chekhov to his fellow writers'.

Although it had earned him a B.Litt. Oxon—the most respected degree in the Faculty of Mediaeval and Modern Languages and Literature—this book is in no sense a dry dissertation: it is a work of love. Gerhardie's love of Chehov is part of his love of life, for what he singles out above all else in Chehov's stories and plays is their complex feel of life as opposed to that neatness by which we usually recognize fiction. Most writers, he argues, produce either introspective fiction at the expense of the visible world; or romantic fiction expressing the smooth dreamy side of life divorced from material reality; or again they produce 'realistic' fiction, employing real material facts with the smooth directness only possible in a romance. But 'it is in the balance of these three elements that gives his [Chehov's] work a lifelike touch, removes him altogether from the musty flavour of tradition which attaches to the sedate profession of letters. When we read Chehov we somehow forget all literary associations. It is as if, forsaking our various professions, we stepped aside to get a better view of life.'

Such enlightened enthusiasm makes for the best kind of criticism, full of extraordinary subtleties, of knowledge and mystery joined in a way that only love can divine. 'It is an excitement and a warmth in the mind that linger for months after reading,' wrote Christopher Morley describing his feelings for this book in *The Romany Stain*. 'It fulfils that beautiful truth that Mr Gerhardie (in his Chehov book) laid down—"A work of art whose aim and meaning were quite clear to the writer in the act of writing it would perish as the universe would perish if its aim were clearly known to it".'

Anton Chehov deals with the whole of Chehov's work, and that part of it concerned with the dramatist should be read by everyone interested in modern drama. In a crucial passage, Gerhardie explains how Chehov resurrects the complete illusion of life 'by using a totally different kind of plot, the tissues of which, as in life, lie below the surface of events, and, unobtrusive, shape our destiny . . . [and] by choosing for his themes stories which were not of the unlikely kind (because taken from real life and developed into "stories"), but just as they would probably have happened if allowed to run their natural course in real life.'

Stanislavsky's much-vaunted 'Method' was, in Gerhardie's view, far too artificial a contrivance for Chehov's plays and achieved little more than stultifying the acting through the regimentation of a ringmaster over-rehearsing his cast to the point of lifeless insensibility. In this it had a result directly opposed to the spirit of Chehov: that of forcing the life out of the plays. Chehov himself was convinced that

Stanislavsky never really read his plays, his chief concern being how he could alter them. But it was Gerhardie who first indentified Stanislavsky as Chehov's prime enemy. In *The Times* and elsewhere, he exposed him for his gross emotional impropriety in cutting out the most telling, the most shattering conclusion of the *Three Sisters*, when Tusenbach is carried in on a stretcher, killed; and deplored his tacking on of all sorts of ludicrous and unnecessary scenes, such as candelabra falling off the ceiling while people are dancing overhead in *The Cherry Orchard*.

The only way to judge a poet, Wordsworth has said, is to love him. It is this love, this deep understanding by one imaginative writer of another, that finally gives Gerhardie's *Chehov* its endearing and enduring quality. The book is an interpretation and a celebration of Chehov's genius, communicating all his miraculous naturalness without that sorry echo of the consumptive's cough. Seldom have scholarship and entertainment, argument and illustration been so happily combined. To some extent, Gerhardie writes, 'literature like his may take the place of actual experience, without the physical exertion, sacrifices, inconvenience, and pain that is inseparable from the business of living; and when they die [readers of Chehov] they may congratulate themselves on having lived a hundred lives—but paid for one'.

It is here that Gerhardie repays his debt to Chehov in life with a small gem of literature.

MICHAEL HOLROYD

ANTON CHEHOV

CHAPTER ONE

THE EFFECT OF HIS WORK, ITS PECULIAR UNIQUENESS

&I

THERE is an experience familiar to travellers. You sit at the train window, and the train shoots through the approaches of some big town, and you see tall squalid houses with the washing hanging out of the window, or perhaps a carpet being beaten in the yard; and your thoughts shoot back to those houses, carpets, linen, and the people living in their atmosphere. How strange, you think, that what is alien to you should be to them the very fibre of existence. And you become aware of the diversity of life, and of your hopeless handicap in keeping pace with it—life is too big, too quick, too varied—and of your puny, puny self.

The approach is from without (involving the particular thrill described); the experience, from within: it is we who live these hitherto unsuspected lives with the acuteness, with the privacy, indeed, of reminiscence. We say as we read Chehov: 'How true to our own experience!' But we are living new, undiscovered lives. How is it? Because in truth there seems nothing that Chehov does not know. And the test? The test is that the truth that there is nothing that *we* do not know does not occur to us till we are reading him, and then we say: 'How true to life.' Why? It may be that, accustomed to a cruder literature and cruder intercourse, we deemed irrational, irrelevant thought as in some manner 'illegitimate,' perverse—a sort of growth confined to our own eccentric self, and so kept it back on the subconscious threshold. How deceived we were as to its importance. For life is more complex, fluid and elusive, not than we had privately suspected (for potentially in a semi-conscious, inarticulate way, we are all of us profoundly subtle), but than we had expected to be told by others, much less to see in print. One of the chief delights of reading Chehov is the discovery that our vaguely apprehended, half-suspected thoughts concerning the fluidness, complexity and elusiveness of life have been confirmed articulately and in print.

It is as if all along we had suspected that the private and unnoticed little things in life were the important ones; but had thought it necessary to present ourselves to our fellows in a stiff intellectual shirt-front. Chehov has eased our joints with candour. To-day it is more difficult to pretend, more difficult to keep up an attitude of insincerity in literature, to affect a thing—even if your affectation be sincerity, a professed dislike of affectation! For this modern literature has the great Russian novelists to thank. The individual 'feel' of living must have been essentially the same for many ages back. It is impossible to credit that the inner, private life of our ancestors was quite as smooth and simple and direct as it was handed down to us in the fiction of their day, with its somewhat formal, as if 'dressed up,' emotion. Where is the documentary evidence of their reactions to the subconscious side of life? Where is their complex inner life, which, if it were anything like our own, must have been strangely at variance with their smooth accounts of it? The older novelists, we suspect, reported life not as it was really lived, but as they thought it *should* be lived, or as they thought that others thought life was, or should be, lived. Perhaps the more rigid rules of life that held them caused them to distrust their inner sense in favour of the accepted forms and standards and conventions; bullied it, in fact, into timid acquiescence. For it is not till one's half-conscious suspicions are encouraged and confirmed by comparison with similar experiences of some one other than oneself that one is at all convinced that one's inner sense of things, discordant as it is with the accepted formal life of fact, is not an idiosyncrasy peculiar to oneself alone, but the real life experienced by every human being. And it is because there is in Chehov's works that fluid undercurrent by which we recognize existence, because we see that he at least did not simplify life in order to round off his picture of it (the loose-end nature of it being just the picture he has set out to portray), and because in a complex version there are necessarily more points of affinity than in a simplified and stripped account of human life, that we recognize ourselves in mental and emotional experiences in point of fact unknown to us.

His is the art of creating convincing illusions of the life that is. And 'the life that is' is what *is* in the material sense of reality, *plus* all the romantic illusions and dreams, *plus* all the sneaking, private, half-conscious perceptions, suspicions, sensations that go side by side with the 'official,' barren life of fact. It is the wanton incompatibility of the reality of life with our romantic, smoother private visions of what life ought to be, and that, together, makes our life seem what it is, with its makeshifts, self-deception, contradiction, and emotional misunderstanding of individual and mutual sensibilities, which has seized him, and, because he saw beauty in it, has made him a creative artist.

How did he come to see beauty in it? Because, I think, he must have felt: now that is life; but somehow we expected, and go on expecting, in defiance of reality, that life ought to be more: we sense a kind of absolute beauty which is more like a song or a poem—'romantic'—and this is the comic pathos of our falling short of it. Why is there a decided sense of beauty about a child cherishing illusions? Why is there a pathetic beauty about the child losing those illusions? Why is there beauty in that tale of his about the little cobbler's boy [*Vanka Zshukov*], who, because he was home-sick and ill-treated at the shop, wrote a letter to his grandfather in the village begging him to take him home at any cost, and after dropping the letter, addressed 'To grandfather in the country,' into the pillar-box, had happy dreams? Why? Unless it be that the inadequacy of what *is* throws the dream of that which ought to be into relief. We are born with a sense of paradise in us. Perhaps we do not go there, and it is only as though we had come from there.

And this perpetual dissatisfaction with herself and everyone else, this series of crude mistakes which stand up like a mountain before one whenever one looks upon one's past, she would accept as her real life to which she was fated, and she would expect nothing better... Of course there was nothing better! Beautiful nature, dreams, music, told one story, but reality another. Evidently truth and happiness existed somewhere outside real life. [*At Home.*]

'Let me remind you,' he writes in a letter, 'that the writers who, we say, are for all time or are simply good, and who intoxicate us, have one common and very important characteristic: they are all going towards something and are summoning you towards it too, and you feel, not with your mind, but with your whole being, that they have some object . . . The best of them are realistic and paint life as it is, but, through every line's being soaked in the consciousness of an object, you feel, besides life as it is, the life which ought to be, and that captivates you.' This is the precise quality of Chehov's own writing—not less so because, in a moment of depression, in his letter he laments the absence of these laudable characteristics from the writing of himself and his contemporaries. He, even more distinctly than his predecessors, makes us feel that he is going out and drawing us 'towards something' transcendental.

The sense of living is a several-fold experience consisting, as it were, of several layers of perception. We recognize life when we sense it. And the reason that so often we do not recognize life in the books that we read is, apart from any question of skill on the part of the writer, because one or more of the 'layers' of perception having been omitted by him, our sense of life is incomplete, impaired—not representative of life's flavour as we know it. Such writing, whatever its other merits, is less rich, if not less true. 'Romantic' fiction, therefore, expressing the smooth dreamy side of life divorced from most material reality; the so-called 'realistic' fiction employing real material facts with the smooth directness only possible in a romance, and, while ignoring the irrational dreamy side of life, flattering itself naïvely on being 'true to life' and 'realistic'; and, lastly, 'introspective' fiction, 'top-heavy' in so far as the detail of its means tends to exceed its own artistic end, are each necessarily poorer, *thinner* than the balanced combination of their elements. And it is this balance of the three elements that gives his work a life-like touch, removes him altogether from the musty flavour of tradition which attaches to the sedate profession of letters. When we read Chehov we somehow forget all literary associations. It is as if, forsaking our various professions, we stepped aside to get a better view of life. And then it seems as if all other men of letters who lived on literature had done no more than step aside, henceforth to walk outside and beside life. Chehov is indeed more than life in the sense that he is the quintessence of it. One forgets that it is books he is writing, that, like others, he must wield a pen, use words; the medium seems accidental. He is concerned with life, with the whole of life since the particular is unsatisfying, with the particular because the whole of life cannot be focused into vividness; and the particular which must needs exclude alternatives reminds him of what he is missing.

'" Why are thy songs so short?" a bird was once asked. " Is it because thou art short of breath?"

'" I have very many songs, and I should like to sing them all."'

This fragment from Daudet is jotted down in one of Chehov's note-books. And certainly it is all but useless to classify his subject-matter. It encompasses all kinds of Russian life that one can think of; and it is the consummative variety of his works remembered as a whole that fills one with a mingled sense of wonder and of lost opportunities—a sense which springs from the realization of the vast variety of existence, impossible to experience since life is given but once, and stingily at that. It is in the essence of things that our appetite tends to increase in proportion to our knowledge of the things we miss, must needs go on doing so. But we do not propose to slacken our pace for all that, and readers of Chehov may perhaps console themselves, because, to some extent at all events, literature like his may take the place of actual experience, without the physical exertion, sacrifices, inconvenience, and pain that is inseparable from the business of living; and when they die they may congratulate themselves on having lived a hundred lives—but paid for one!

Progression means a succession of lost opportunities. And this is where Chehov grips us. The element that makes for his disquieting appeal is determined by this phenomenon. But to call him a pessimist is absurd. Nevertheless, this view of him is often held, not only by persons upon whom it is forced by the inevitable inadequacy of translations, but equally by those who read him in his native tongue. Perhaps progression as interpreted above would scarcely appear a cheerful proposition. It is a series of 'farewells,' sad, if you will, but yet inevitable, and beautiful because of their inherent quality of cosmic inevitability. The pessimistic attitude towards such phenomena would be one of whining at the failing in our common nature—an attitude extreme, crippled, and one-sided. Because it is unjust to life. For we are not even able to imagine the alternative of a transitory existence. To rebel against it, therefore, would be unjust. It would, as a practical proposition, be absurd. Chehov, though the melancholy beauty of his plays and stories is the melancholy of a transitory world, cannot be called a pessimist, in the face of the ridiculous implication of such an attitude. A pessimistic attitude would mean that he had no sense of proportion; and it is perhaps the chief determining cause of his sensibility that he had, if ever a man had, a perfect sense of proportion. The optimistic attitude, on the other hand, being uncalled for by the delusive nature of happiness, is not altogether his either. For, says Colonel Vershinin in the *Three Sisters*: 'Recently I have been reading the diary of a certain French cabinet minister, written while he was in prison. With what rapture, what joy, he alludes to the birds he sees through the prison window, which he hadn't noticed while he was a minister. Now that he is released, of course, as before, he doesn't notice the birds. So you won't notice Moscow, when you come to live in it. We have no happiness, and there *is* none; we only long for it.' It is better to dream of paradise than to go there. For when you know you cease to care. Happiness, as we learn in retrospect, is when we feel we have a heaven in reserve. It was not apathy alone that kept the three sisters from embarking on the train to Moscow, but a suspicion deep down in their hearts that the climax coming at the end of the crescendo is generally somewhat disappointing. For lack of any further heaven in reserve. And this needs must be so, since there seems no existence outside motion. The stationary nature of happiness is a delusion. Faust wished he could say to a single moment: '*Verweile doch, du bist so schön!*' It was an impossible demand; a contradiction in terms; a negation of life, and with it of beauty. Chehov was neither pessimist nor optimist. To him life is neither horrible nor happy, but unique, strange, fleeting, beautiful and awful.

And all the time, while life is passing, always you can feel in him that aching isolation of the individual soul. 'As I shall lie in the grave alone, so in fact I live alone,' is a thought jotted down in his note-book. His gay, companionable people laugh, but live alone. And mutely, by the mere fact of their presence upon earth, each seems to put a question.

'Yes, no one knows the real truth . . .' thought Laevski, looking wearily at the dark, restless sea. [*The Duel.*]

'It flings the boat back,' he thought; 'she makes two steps forward and one step back; but the boatmen are stubborn, they work the oars unceasingly, and are not afraid of the high waves. The boat goes on and on. Now she is out of sight, but in half an hour the boatmen will see the steamer lights distinctly, and within an hour they will be by the steamer ladder. So it is in life... In the search for truth man makes two steps forward and one step back. Suffering, mistakes, and weariness of life thrust them back, but the thirst for truth and stubborn will drive them on and on. And who knows? Perhaps they will reach the real truth at last.'

And it would seem as if the whole significance of life reposed on the validity of that 'perhaps.'

& II

It is his sense of justice that is at the back of his discriminating faculty. In *Enemies* he writes:

The doctor stood, leaning with one hand on the edge of the table, and looked at Abogin with that profound and somewhat cynical, ugly contempt only to be found in the eyes of sorrow and indigence when they are confronted with well-nourished comfort and elegance.

. . . All the way home the doctor thought not of his wife, not of his Andrei, but of Abogin and the people in the house he had just left. His thoughts were unjust and inhumanly cruel. He condemned Abogin and his wife and Papchinski and all who lived in rosy, subdued light among sweet perfumes, and all the way home he hated and despised them till his head ached. And a firm conviction concerning those people took shape in his mind.

Time will pass and Kirilov's sorrow will pass, but that conviction, unjust and unworthy of the human heart, will not pass, but will remain in the doctor's mind to the grave.

In his note-book there is this delightful fragment, which is like a comical pendant to the idea expressed in *Enemies*:

The nobleman X. sold his estate to N. with all the furniture, stock, etc., but he took away everything else, even the oven dampers, and after that N. hated all noblemen.

Human nature, he perceives, is sometimes subtle to an extraordinary degree, if analysed. And yet the experience which in literature we hail as remarkable is possibly familiar to us in real life. Solëni in the *Three Sisters* is said to be quite a good and sensible fellow provided he is alone with you, but in the company of other people he becomes unspeakably silly. He constantly comes up to Baron Tusenbach, with whom he is on very friendly terms when they are alone, and engages in significant but meaningless remarks, for no reason at all—or because he is shy and somewhat bored. A similar discernment shows in a jotting in one of Chehov's note-books. X. and Z., who are good friends, begin, immediately they meet each other in the company of others, to chaff each other a little viciously—out of shyness. Possibly the idea which he first jotted down in his note-book as it occurred to him he subsequently realized in the *Three Sisters*. At any rate, it is very delightful. No doubt the average intelligent person is aware of making similar discoveries in the course of the routine of life (or it would not occur to him to applaud the thing when seen in print). But the average intelligence does not usually communicate these subtle observations to another, much less set them down in writing. In the average mind the discovery scarcely assumes the shape of words. It comes and goes, leaving no impression. And it is the expression of it that is a nerve-racking experience, or, as Mr. Arnold Bennett once put it: 'It is the *writing* which hastens death.'

At least one-half of Chehov's attitude to life was humorous. Apart from his farces, his humour was of that high comedic quality: never quite divorced from a suspicion of tragedy. It is warm and human.

An example from his note-book:

N. tells how forty years ago X., a wonderful and extraordinary man, had saved the lives of five people, and N. feels it strange that every one listened with indifference, that the history of X. is already forgotten and uninteresting.

In the rough draft of the *Three Sisters* the schoolmaster, a self-sufficient bore, says: 'I'm a jolly fellow. I infect every one with my mood.' He is Màsha's husband. Irina, Màsha's sister, comments: 'Màsha's out of sorts to-day. She married when she was eighteen, when he seemed to her the wisest of men. And now it's different. He's the kindest man, but not the wisest.' And towards the end of the drama, when the sensitive, discriminating sisters are deeply moved and melancholy, the rather stupid optimistic schoolmaster holds forth: 'But I've been lucky all my life. I'm happy, and I even have the Stanislaus Cross, second grade... Of course, I'm a clever man, much cleverer than many, but happiness doesn't only lie in that.'

On Irina's birthday he gives her a present: 'It's the history of our High School during the last fifty years, written by myself. In this book you will find a list of all those who have taken the full course at our High School during these last fifty years.' The humour is indeed comi-tragic!

To take a few more examples from his note-books:

He had nothing in his soul except recollections of his school-days as a cadet.

He hoped to win two hundred thousand in a lottery, twice in succession, because two hundred thousand would not be enough for him.

A certain captain taught his daughter the art of fortification.

A schoolboy treats a lady to dinner in a restaurant. He has only one rouble twenty copecks. The bill comes to four roubles thirty copecks. He has no money and begins to cry. The proprietor boxes his ears. He was talking to the lady about Abyssinia.

He learnt Swedish [Norwegian?] in order to study Ibsen, spent a lot of time and trouble, and suddenly realized that Ibsen was not important; he could not conceive what use he could now make of the Swedish language.

A Government clerk gave his son a thrashing because he had only obtained five marks in all his subjects at school. It seemed to him not good enough. When he was told that he was in the wrong, that five is the highest mark obtainable, he thrashed his son again—out of vexation with himself.

A young man collected a million stamps, lay down on them, and shot himself.

'Your fiancée is very pretty.' 'To me all women are alike.'

An old man of eighty says to another old man of sixty: 'You ought to be ashamed, young man.'

In the daytime conversations about the loose manners of the girls in secondary schools, in the evening a lecture on degeneration and the decline of everything, and at night, after all this, one longs to shoot oneself.

It has been said that some of the items jotted down in Chehov's note-books are trashy. Well they might be, since they were meant to be put into the mouths of trashy people. When Chehov wants to lapse into the minor key he selects material that borders on the humorous. Olga tells Irina that when the Baron left the army and came to them in plain clothes she began crying because he seemed so bad-looking. [*Three Sisters.*] He asked her why she was crying. How could she tell him? Natàsha, Andrei's fiancée, who is reproved by Olga, and commented upon by Màsha, for the way she dresses, in her turn three years afterwards reproves Irina for her belt, which she describes as 'an error of taste.' From the timid fiancée that she had been in the first act, Natàsha, when she marries Andrei, gradually, through a kind of peaceful penetration, becomes mistress of the household. She is just a little vulgar, but she does not see it, and actually reproves Màsha for her fresh and boisterous language, which to Natàsha's unsuspecting soul appears indelicate! She, whose genteel provincialism grates on the others, apes the manners of the nobility, and interjects in French (a practice condoned some thirty years before, but, by the time she has adopted it, already looked upon as a little vulgar by the nobility itself): '*Je vous prie, pardonnez-moi, Marie, mais vous avez des manières un peu grossières.*' And the Baron, trying to restrain his laughter, mutters: 'Give me . . . give me . . . there's some cognac, I think.'

Her character is drawn in a masterly way, but so are all the characters in the *Three Sisters*; and it is interesting to note how by their separate attitude to her another shade of difference in the characters of the three sisters is revealed. The dialogue between Olga and Natàsha on the question of the servant is a marvellously illuminating piece of character drawing. Indeed, one suspects that Chehov must have been aware that a mutual reluctance on the part of his characters to appreciate or understand each other's attitude or feeling inevitably enhances the sympathetic understanding and the sensibility of the audience. Thus, when the three sisters tell the Colonel of the wonders of the life in Moscow, whither they are longing to go back, the Colonel, who has just arrived from there, declares that their provincial town is far superior in climate and surroundings.

Or take this extract from the *Cherry Orchard*:

The servant-girl Dunyasha is dying to tell her young mistress, who has only just arrived from Paris, that she had been proposed to: 'I must tell you at once. I can't bear to wait a minute.'

ANYA (*tired*). At it again...

DUNYASHA. The clerk Epihodov proposed to me after Easter.

ANYA. You're always at the same. (*Puts her hair straight.*) I've lost all my hairpins. (*She is very tired, even sways as she walks.*)

DUNYASHA. I don't know what to think about it. He loves me, loves me so much!

ANYA (*looks into her room; tenderly*). My room, my windows, just as if I'd never gone away. I'm at home!

& III

Like Turgenev, he speaks of 'that eternal repose of "indifferent nature,"' of 'eternal reconciliation and of life everlasting':

At Oreanda they sat on a seat not far from the church, looked down at the sea, and were silent. Yalta was hardly visible through the morning mist; white clouds stood motionless on the mountain-tops. The leaves did not stir on the trees, grasshoppers chirruped, and the monotonous hollow sound of the sea, rising up from below, spoke of the peace, of the eternal sleep awaiting us. So it must have sounded when there was no Yalta, no Oreanda here; so it sounds now, and it will sound as indifferently and monotonously when we are all no more. And in this constancy, in this complete indifference to the life and death of each of us, there lies hid, perhaps, a pledge of our eternal salvation, of the unceasing movement of life upon earth, of unceasing progress towards perfection. Sitting beside a young woman who in the dawn seemed so lovely, soothed and spell-bound in these magical surroundings—the sea, mountains, clouds, the open sky—Gurov thought how in reality everything is beautiful in this world when one reflects: everything except what we think or do ourselves when we forget our human dignity and the higher aims of our existence. [*The Lady with the Dog.*]

His intuition draws him on towards the mystery of cosmic transitoriness, sensible behind the personal tragedy of loss:

That repellent horror which is thought of when we speak of death was absent from the room. In the numbness of everything, in the mother's attitude, in the indifference on the doctor's face, there was something that attracted and touched the heart, that subtle, almost elusive beauty of human sorrow which men will not for a long time learn to understand and describe, and which it seems only music can convey. There was a feeling of beauty, too, in the austere stillness. Kirilov and his wife were silent and not weeping, as though besides the bitterness of their loss they were conscious, too, of all the tragedy of their position; just as once their youth had passed away, so now together with this boy their right to have children had gone for ever to all eternity! [*Enemies.*]

And why this sense of tranquil beauty behind the bitterness of loss—as though there were some unknown justification in the seeming wantonness of it? A hidden harmony. What is it? And then in this fragment, found after his death, there is a hint that he is tapping with his pen the very source and justification of life's transitoriness—its simultaneous diversity:

> Essentially all this is crude and meaningless, and romantic love appears as meaningless as an avalanche which involuntarily rolls down a mountain and overwhelms people. But when one listens to music, all this is—that some people lie in their graves and sleep, and that one woman is alive and, grey-haired, is now sitting in a box in the theatre, seems quiet and majestic, and the avalanche no longer meaningless, since in nature everything has a meaning. And everything is forgiven, and it would be strange not to forgive.

To him there is a meaning in the high indifference of nature to the ultimate importance of our ego; justification of all life in the balance of obliteration; mercy and stability in the ultimate release of the individual soul; and forgiveness in the thought that eventually no individual deed will matter individually. And by that indifference the very trivialities of life are balanced, and the stability transfigured with a meaning, 'since in nature everything has a meaning. And everything is forgiven, and it would be strange not to forgive.'

CHAPTER TWO

THE SENSIBILITY WHICH NECESSITATED THIS EXPRESSION

&I

'I AM AFRAID of those who look for a tendency between the lines, and who are determined to regard me either as a liberal or as a conservative,' Chehov writes in a letter:

> I am not a liberal, not a conservative, not a believer in gradual progress, not a monk, not an indifferentist. I should like to be a free artist and nothing more, and I regret that God has not given me the power to be one. I hate lying and violence in all their forms... Pharisaism, stupidity, and despotism reign not in merchants' houses and prisons alone. I see them in science, in literature, in the younger generation... That is why I have no preference either for gendarmes, or for butchers, or for scientists, or for writers, or for the younger generation. I regard trade-marks and labels as a superstition. My holy of holies is the human body, health, intelligence, talent, inspiration, love, and the most absolute freedom—freedom from violence and lying, whatever forms they may take. This is the programme I would follow if I were a great artist.

He is impatient of generalities masquerading as progress. 'If you cry "Forward!"' is a thought found among other fragments after his death, 'you must without fail explain in which direction one must go. Do you not see that, if, without explaining the direction, you fire off this word simultaneously at a monk and at a revolutionary, they will proceed in precisely opposite directions?' But he is ever anxious to avoid any wasteful conflict that results from hollow watchwords. 'I want people not to see war where there is none,' he writes in a letter. . . ' When a man fails to understand something, he is conscious of a discord, and seeks for the cause of it, not in himself, as he should, but outside himself—hence the war with what he does not understand. In the Middle Ages alchemy was gradually in a natural, peaceful way changing into chemistry, and astrology into astronomy; the monks did not understand, saw a conflict, and fought against it.'

Here are two illuminating extracts from his abortive diary:

> Between ' there is a God ' and ' there is no God ' there lies a whole vast field, which a true sage traverses with great difficulty. A Russian only knows one of the two extremities, but the middle in between does not interest him; and that is why he generally knows nothing, or very little.

Again:

> The ease with which Hebrews change their faith is justified by many by their indifference. But this is no justification. One should also respect one's indifference and change it for nothing else, for in a good man indifference is the very same religion.

' Nature,' he writes in a letter, ' is an excellent sedative. It pacifies—that is, it makes one indifferent. And it is essential in this world to be indifferent. Only those who are indifferent are able to see things clearly, to be just and to work. Of course, I am only speaking of intelligent people of fine natures; the empty and selfish are indifferent anyway.' But such ' indifference ' exacts proportionately heavy dues in return for its seeming aloofness, and it exacts them, paradoxically enough, in that acute sensitiveness which is the consequence of an intellectual *impasse*. So much so, that, cornered by his always present sense of practical absurdity, he can advance but one possible explanation of his intellectual condition—that it is a temporary phase in the evolution of civilization, a sort of a disease for which he is not himself to blame, of which, moreover, it is not for him to cure himself, 'for this disease,' he says, 'it must be supposed, has some good purpose hidden from us, and is not sent in vain.' It is, we must suppose, a cog in the wheels of transcendence.

For him life and literature resolve into a perpetual finding and refinding of the balance between the end and means of life; and well may his friend Suvorin write to complain that his work lacked 'alcohol,' was, indeed, 'lemonade.' Chehov realized that holy wars waged in the name of fairness, impartiality, and peace would be better for being less holy and less war-like. But, waged reluctantly, with deference to the enemy, in a spirit of fair play and ready understanding, wars are in danger of ceasing to be wars. Hence the 'lemonade.' And he confesses: 'We have neither immediate nor remote aims, and in our soul there is a great empty space. We have no politics, we do not believe in revolution, we have no God. . . Flog us and we can do no more!' 'Mankind used to be absorbed in wars,' says Colonel Vershinin in the *Three Sisters*, 'and all its existence was filled with campaigns, attacks, victories; now we've outlived all that, leaving after us a great waste place, which there is nothing to fill with at present; but mankind is passionately looking for something, and will certainly find it. Ah, if it only happened more quickly. If only education could be added to industry, and industry to education.'

Imagine Mr. Shaw being perpetually contradicted by Mr. Chesterton, and the resulting neutralization is approximately what has been going on in Chehov's mind. Imagine the revolutionary and the monk both shouting 'Forward!' in the mind of a single man, and you will not be astonished at Chehov's choice of standing still. Imagine two able advocates completely neutralizing each other in the conscience of one individual, and you will not be surprised at his reluctance to pronounce judgment on his fellows. There is a terror hidden in it, a kind of a metaphysical dismay, that lends his work a very peculiar flavour. Essentially he had no axe to grind. I remember Mr. Middleton Murry stressing this point in a lecture he gave at Oxford some two years ago. But when I write that Chehov was 'terrified' of the 'great waste place' created temporarily by our having outgrown the illusions and ideals of previous generations, I do not imply that he slept any the less soundly for that knowledge. It must be remembered that his sense of humour, which was delicate and keen to an extraordinary degree, invariably stepped in to preserve his intellectual balance. There are numerous instances in his plays and stories of his delight in the portrayal of persons of both sexes 'dissatisfied with their surroundings and seeking a purpose in life,' and the calculated comic touch of it is shrewd enough: he is laughing mischievously at their ridiculous immodesty in airing such pretensions. There is something of his lying cook about them, who boasts, cigarette in mouth: 'I studied at a high school. I knows what for the earth is round.' [*Note-book.*] The kind of thing I mean is sometimes met with in a child's experience, who discovers for the first time in its life that the toys are 'only toys,' that there is nothing whatsoever 'real' about them. The discovery is devastating. In politics this feeling must be experienced by men of intellectual honesty and imagination at a time when the opposing parties become identical in ideal and aim. It is a sense which leaves you desolate for want of a motive. But Chehov learnt to overcome it in his art. He tumbles to the ingenious idea of harnessing this artistically mortifying sense of intellectual impotence and desolation to artistic ends. The want of motive is his artistic motive. And in his crowning work, the *Three Sisters*, his achievement is complete.

But in the face of his professed 'indifference' and in the face of his professed 'disease' there is a conspicuous abundance of contradictory symptoms. There is his always active faculty of observation, there is his passion for dispassion, and a healthy zest of living amply overtopping any gloomy moods. If Chehov had no axe to grind, he ground it, none the less so, to a razor-blade of perpetual discrimination. In one of his letters he comments on *War and Peace*. 'I wake up every night and read "War and Peace,"' he writes:

> One reads it with the same interest and naïve wonder as though one had never read it before. It's amazingly good. Only I don't like the passages in which Napoleon appears. As soon as Napoleon comes on the scene, there are forced explanations and tricks of all sorts to prove that he was stupider than he really was. Everything that is said and done by Pierre, Prince Andrei, or the absolutely insignificant Nikolai Rostov—all that is good, clever, natural, and touching; everything that is thought and done by Napoleon is not natural, not clever, inflated, and worthless.

This sense of the 'great waste place' is caused by an intellectual reluctance towards partisan decision. He spots prejudice wherever it may manifest itself. 'Tolstoy calls our having money and eating meat lying,' he writes in a letter; 'that's too much... Tolstoy denies mankind immortality, but, my God! how much that is personal there is in it!... The devil take the philosophy of the great ones of this world! All the great sages are as despotic as generals, and as ignorant and as indelicate as generals, because they feel secure of impunity.' At the same time, to him people are at once more simple and more subtle than his most complex definitions of them, which their living personalities somehow defy. Here is an illuminating extract from his story, *The Wife*:

> I listened to the doctor, and, according to my habit, applied my usual measures to him—materialist, idealist, money-grubber, herd-instincts, and so forth, but not a single of my measures would fit even approximately; and, curiously, while I only listened to him and looked at him, he was, as a man, perfectly clear to me, but the moment I began applying my measures to him he became, despite all his sincerity and simplicity, an extraordinarily complex, confused, and inexplicable nature.

(And it is the former attitude, as distinct from the latter attitude indulged in by Henry James, that determines Chehov's simple method of conveying subtleties on paper. But to this I shall return in a later chapter.)

The love-sick Màsha thus confesses to her sister Olga in the *Three Sisters*: 'When you read a novel it all seems so old and easy, but when you fall in love yourself, then you learn that nobody knows anything, and that each must decide for himself.'

Therefore it will be seen that there is no essential inertia or inaction, as had been so frequently asserted, about Chehov's attitude to life.

& II

The real cause of his apparent intellectual weariness lies deeper; it lies in his mistrust of logic. The law of contradiction, by which cruder minds have laid such store, works so well because it naïvely overlooks the fine gradations that lie between its two opposite poles. It must have its Yes *or* No, and is blind to what lies between them. Speculations as to life and death are thrashed out in the same incisive way by the logicians—To be, or not to be—

forgetting that it is only necessary to substitute the word *becoming* for that of *being* (since creation does not take place in the twinkling of an eye out of nothing, but is a matter of involution out of something else) to realize that logic, when it encroaches upon abstract questions, is apt to be rather like a bull in a china-shop. And if the questions that are implied in Chehov's works do not always admit of a logical answer, it is as often as not the fault of logic, which is a mere rule-of-thumb affair—inaccurately precise—when it is confronted by transcendental values. Perhaps in Chehov's mind we may already see an indication of that distant future when the law of contradiction may slowly loose its hold on our mode of thought, as its dams are gradually undermined by the subtler waves of intuitive gradation (if this be in the programme of transcending involution).

'There is not a single criterion which can serve as the measure of the non-existent, of the non-human,' is a thought in his note-book. Thus he rules out non-existence intuitively as effectively as it can be ruled out logically. (The existence of non-existence is a contradiction in terms.) And he leaves us with the anticipation of some middle way, some gradation of consciousness in a universe at once static and transitory, one might almost say 'static' in its absolute transitoriness, just as living is both transitory in so far as the experience of it is determined by change, and static in so far as the continuity of our consciousness seems independent of change—as if we were sitting still in a moving vehicle.

All of which logically is nonsense. But the whole point is that possibly the secret of existence is outside logic. It certainly is not inside it. That we know. By the test of logic life makes nonsense. At any rate, we are entitled to suspect that logic is not all, for two good reasons—because logic leaves out a good deal of our spiritual sense of truth, and because logic cannot explain truth even to its own logical satisfaction.

Life would seem to be a sort of self-expression in an infinite variety of ways, which, for want of a ' first cause ' (which must be ruled out even by the crudely inadequate theory of causation itself), and for want of cosmic choice as to aim, direction, or order of succession, results in chaos : a defiance of continued order, with elusiveness for aim, and so itself a sort of order, fluctuating in the act of cancellation, there being no commanding choice to order its (or an alternative) monopoly, the resulting fluctuation being just that impetus of the *perpetuum mobile* called life. In other words, since there is no reason why life be thus or otherwise, life is *everywise* : a struggle towards the static and simultaneous on the part of the transitory and successive, and towards transition and diversity on the part of the static and uniform (since there is no more warrant for one than the other). Otherwise, if life had an attainable goal (for which there is no warrant), life would be committing suicide the moment that this goal was reached, or even earlier—the moment any of its particles conceived it in advance. For which also there would seem no warrant. Therefore life is an equilibrium of transitory values, whereas what is absolute and static is perhaps its equilibrium.

But this is merely an endeavour to approach Chehov's sensibility by way of a metaphysical speculation (my own for choice). Yet while mistrusting the efficacy of logic, particularly in metaphysics, he was deterred by the futility of breaking through those walls. There was, moreover, no earthly reason why logic should not last its time. The value of intuitive gradation was in its gradual realization : it was nothing if it was not gradual. And thus he felt that there was nothing for him to get excited about either in the matter of religion, or of metaphysics, or of philosophy, or of literature. His contribution was an attitude of discrimination towards life, and he knew that in due course civilization will have made use of it. His contemplation of Fyodor Dostoevski banging at the walls for all he was worth did not particularly impress him. He writes in a letter that such questions as free-will, predestination, and non-resistance to evil can only be settled in the future. But now and then, when tired of walking round and round in the round cell of reason, Chehov too would stop and gently bang the wall and listen to the hollow sound. Yes, it seemed as though there was something behind the prison wall of reason, after all.

And it seems that in another little while we shall know why we are alive, why we have to suffer. [*Three Sisters.*]

& III

A philosophical, indeed a metaphysical, attitude was always present at the back of Chehov's mind. But if he was not, in practice, a philosopher, it is because in philosophy, if, in the phrase of Mr. Wells, you are to 'lift hand and brain and say, "I too will add,"' you must travel *forward* at least some little distance. But to go out any distance means keeping to one road and being blind to the existence of all other roads. And all roads do not necessarily lead to a common destination. It is true enough that you can only take one road at a time if you are to get anywhere at all. But having got wherever it may be, you begin to doubt whether it is truth that you have reached. For what of all the other roads? you ask. Is that which in its blindness overlooks nine out of ten of them the *whole* truth even if it be the *only* truth? And if the latter, may it not be arrogance rather than truth?

Truth is an enemy of definition. And the fault is that of definition. And this is where the novelist has the clear advantage over the philosopher. The writer does not in the least concern himself with definitions. The writer need not, if he has a clear idea of the advantage of his craft, avail himself of the philosopher's disadvantage. He is a fool if he does. Or he is a bad writer. The writer need not, must not, walk up any single road towards truth; for that way he will never get there. The writer, if he is an artist, can largely dispense with logic (which is the philosopher's only tool); at any rate, a writer must subordinate logic to something which is more valuable, as a vehicle of spiritual truth. His sensibility must draw him to express truth, where logic by itself is helpless; must draw him to express it intuitively, instinctively. A writer, like a painter, or a composer, can reach out towards truth, and capture it for a few moments, by sitting on the cross-roads. A philosopher cannot escape the peril of walking up one road, which, being one out of so many, whichever it may be, will turn out to be the wrong one.

In my laboured attempts to analyse the metaphysical undercurrent of Chehov's sensibility I have stretched the meaning of language to the breaking-point. In my endeavour to define the possible non-existence of contradiction outside human criterions I had to contradict myself a dozen times. Definition capitulates. But what I have been trying to express through logic has been expressed by Chehov in the passage I have quoted:

But when one listens to music, all this is—that some people lie in their graves and sleep, and that one woman is alive and, grey-haired, is now sitting in a box in the theatre, seems quiet and majestic, and the avalanche [romantic love] no longer meaningless, since in nature everything has a meaning. And everything is forgiven, and it would be strange not to forgive.

It has the double advantage over my efforts to define the simultaneous effect of life's diversity that it is beautiful and that it is shorter. And it has the additional advantage of succeeding in expressing some elusive quality of truth which I could not express at all.

& IV

I do not presume that I could give the whole of Chehov's outlook in a nutshell. But if pressed to do so, I would rather say that Chehov's outlook in a nutshell was that he thoroughly distrusted nutshells. His intellectual attitude was inconclusive. After he has said his say, there is still the implication that he reserves the right to leave his further thoughts unsaid, even unthought. And this can be understood. It is the cruder writers with undigested things to say who like to end on a conclusive note. Their passion sees them through. Whereas Chehov's passion is a passion for dispassion. It sees him through in his process of digesting life—a process to which, however, there is no proper ending. He ends upon an inconclusive note: indeed, so far as it is his aim to demonstrate that truth is in its very nature inconclusive, he ends on a conclusive note.

'It is time that writers,' he says in a letter, 'especially those who are artists, recognized that there is no making out anything in this world, as once Socrates recognized it, and Voltaire too.'

The mob thinks it knows and understands everything; and the more stupid it is, the wider it imagines its outlook to be. And if a writer whom the mob believes in has the courage to say that he does not understand anything of what he sees, that alone will be something gained in the realm of thought and a great step in advance.

So long as scepticism means (by M. Anatole France's definition) merely a denial of negations, Chehov may be said to be a sceptic in his outlook. (That he feared and hated labels does not in itself exempt him from such labels.) He is very much aware of our mental limitations, and consequently of our hopeless handicap in trying to envisage truth by mental means alone. And he is a sceptic in so far as he suspects philosophers who claim to have captured truth by circumscription of being blind to all the other truth that they have left outside. But 'truth,' 'reason,' 'God,' are confusing terms, and require separate definition on each occasion of their use. Let me, therefore, illustrate exactly what I mean by truth and reason so far as they here concern him. Reason is a sort of a balloon wherein we dwell: you can stretch it at any point you like, but you will have tampered with its natural round shape. Progress in philosophy can be achieved with ease by impairing, as it were, the symmetry of reason at any of its points—by stretching truth. And since Chehov would not recognize as truth any angular conception of it, it would seem that mentally there was nothing left for him but to wander round, like a fly inside a globe, and to discover as it were that truth, for all mental purposes, was a round globe in which he was confined, and, after gaining the conviction of its irrevocable roundness, to tumble to the bright idea that the greater part of truth may be outside the globe of reason. It is only natural that after that his wanderings inside should come to a permanent halt. His case is: Why break your skull over a minor riddle if it is but a portion of a major one, which we can dimly feel but not define? And that he can convey his sense of spiritual truth intuitively into his pages is his one escape from the *impasse* of reason. It is like the calmness which underlies the surface ripples of a restless lake.

But—to have a last go at the image—if reason is comparable to a balloon wherein we dwell, and if the stretching of it at any point would illustrate unreason, so the blowing of it up to an ever larger size would cover such mental progress as is achieved, for instance, by research work. For Chehov had the same belief in ethical and scientific progress as, for example, Mr. Wells. But what he asked himself, and what sometimes he doubted, was whether man at any ultimate stage of his development would be completely able to account for the *raison d'être* of phenomena, and cease to suffer both the anguish of unsatisfied curiosity and the alternative dissatisfaction of *ennui*; whether ever he would get beyond the sense of the *Weltschmerz*. 'Not only after two or three hundred, but in a million years, life will still be as it was,' replies Baron Tusenbach in the *Three Sisters* to Colonel Vershinin, whose thesis is that everything on earth must gradually change, and that some day a new and happy life will begin for mankind; 'life does not change, it remains for ever, following its own laws, which do not concern us, or which, at any rate, you will never find out. Migrant birds—cranes, for example—fly and fly, and whatever thoughts, high or low, enter their heads, they will still fly, and not know why or where. They fly, and will continue to fly, whatever philosophers come to life among them; they may philosophize as much as they like, only they will fly...' To this Màsha rejoins: 'Still, a meaning?' 'A meaning . . .' he says. 'There, it's snowing. What meaning?' And, after a pause, she takes it up: 'It seems to me that man must have faith, or seek faith, or his life is empty, empty... To live and not to know why cranes fly, why babies are born, why there are stars in the sky. . . Either you know what you are living for, or nothing matters.'

Reason will not answer this. And in a fragment found after his death among his papers he shrinks from the fatuity of reasoning:

> So long as a man likes the splashing of a fish, he is a poet; when he knows that the splashing is nothing but the chase of the weak by the strong, he is a thinker; but when he does not understand what sense there is in the chase, or what use in the equilibrium which results from destruction, he is becoming silly and dull, as he was when a child. And the more he knows and thinks, the sillier he becomes.

He questions (and intuitively probes down to a half-answer) what may be the truth outside the exasperating roundness of that balloon of reason when, as we die, it bursts? What may be its 'shape,' then, and will it have a 'shape' such as we, as yet, cannot imagine, or will it have no 'shape'—or be an empty sound? 'You'll die all the same,' says Gaev in the *Cherry Orchard*, in answer to Trofimov's exhortation that man must work for his salvation. 'Who knows?' says Trofimov. 'And what does it mean—"you'll die"? Man may have a hundred senses, of which only the five which are known to us perish with death, and the other ninety-five go on living.' Which implies a gradation of consciousness in a universe dormant, not dead. Whatever death may be, there is a significance, he feels, even in the blackest silence of extinction. For it, too, is but a phase of the diversity of life, of the eternal variation chasing in the direction of elusiveness for want of choice. And thus it is a part of life. 'Here's a tree,' says Baron Tusenbach as he parts with Irina, before the fatal duel, 'which has dried up, but it still sways in the breeze with the others. And so it seems to me that if I die, I shall still take part in life in one way or another.'

✠ V

I sometimes fancy that the God we seek in nature was love incarnate, who, understanding everything, forgave everything, thus loosing His grip upon nature. The happy-go-lucky, line-of-least-resistance, trial-and-error ways of nature would suggest that speculation. And Chehov, like Mr. Wells, stakes his faith (such of it as in moments of optimism he can scrape together) on the 'Spirit of God in Man,' on 'this fire of human tradition we have lit upon this little planet, if it is the one gleam of spirit in all the windy vastness of a dead and empty universe.' I quote from Mr. Wells. Those who speak of Chehov's 'hopelessness' and 'pessimism' should lend an ear to the duet that follows, of which Mr. Wells (I constantly read that Mr. Wells is said to have a high-pitched voice) properly takes the treble. But the tune, it will be seen, is essentially the same.

Says Colonel Vershinin in the *Three Sisters*:

> It seems to me that everything on earth must change, little by little, and is already changing under our very eyes. After two or three hundred years, after a thousand—the actual time doesn't matter—a new and happy age will begin. We, of course, shall not take part in it, but we live and work and even suffer to-day that it should come. We create it—and in that one object is our destiny, and, if you like, our happiness.

Says Mr. Huss in Mr. Wells's *The Undying Fire*:

> Yet there is work to be done by everyone, a plain reason for that work, and happiness in the doing of it... I do not know if any of us realize all that a systematic organization of the human intelligence upon the work of research would mean for our race... We do not realize what in a little while mankind

could do. Our power over matter, our power over life, our power over ourselves, would increase year by year and day by day.

Colonel Vershinin:

In two or three hundred years' time life on this earth will be unimaginably beautiful and wonderful. Mankind needs such a life, and if it is not ours to-day, then we must look ahead for it, wait, think, prepare for it. We must see and know more than our fathers and grandfathers saw and knew.

Mr. Huss:

Is it not plain to you all, from what man, in spite of everything, has achieved, that he is but at the beginning of achievement; that presently he will take his body and his life and mould them to his will; that he will take gladness and beauty for himself as a girl will pick a flower and twine it in her hair?

Colonel Vershinin:

And I wish I could make you understand that there is no happiness for us, that there should not and cannot be... We must only work and work, and happiness is only for our distant posterity... If not for me, then for the descendants of my descendants.

Mr. Huss:

The important thing in us is the least personal thing. It is not you nor I who go on living; it is Man that lives on, Man the Universal, and he goes on living, a tragic rebel in the same world and in no other.

Irina (in the *Three Sisters*):

A time will come when every one will know what all this is about, what all this suffering is for; there will be no more mysteries, but meanwhile we must live . . . work, only work!

Mr. Huss:

There burns an undying fire in the hearts of men. By that fire I live. By that I know the God of my Salvation. His will is

Truth; His will is Service. He urges me to conflict, without consolations, without rewards.

Trofimov (in the *Cherry Orchard*):

Here is happiness, here it comes; nearer and nearer; I hear its steps. And should we not see it, should we not know it, what matter? Others will see it!

Mr. Huss:

He takes and does not restore. He uses up and does not atone. He suffers—perhaps to triumph, and we must suffer and find our hope of triumph in Him. He will not let me shut my eyes to sorrow, failure, or perplexity. Though the universe torment and slay me, yet will I trust in Him. And if He also must die—— Nevertheless I can do no more; I must serve Him.

Chehov (in a letter):

. . . The religious movement of which you write is one thing, and the whole trend of modern culture is another, and one cannot place the second in any causal connexion with the first. . . The religious movement of which we talked is a survival, almost the end of what has ceased, or is ceasing to exist. Modern culture is the first beginning of the work for a great future, work which will perhaps go on for tens of thousands of years, in order that man may, if only in the remote future, come to know the truth of the real God—that is not, I conjecture, by seeking in Dostoevski, but by clear knowledge, as one knows twice two are four.

Mr. Huss:

All this world will man make a garden for himself, ruling not only his kind but all the lives that live, banishing the cruel from life, making the others merciful and tame beneath his hand. The flies and mosquitoes, the thorns and poisons, the fungus in the blood, and the murrain upon his beasts, he will utterly end. He will rob the atoms of their energy and the depths of space of their secrets. He will break his prison in space. He will step from star to star as now we step from stone to stone across a stream. Until he stands in the light of God's presence and looks his Mocker and the Adversary in the face.

There is, it will be seen, no essential difference between the religion of Mr. Wells and Chehov's interpretation of 'modern culture.' It is, to be sure, this 'God in the Human Heart' who, in Mr. Wells's interpretation, 'rises out of your process as if he were a part of your process but who has meaning only for us, to whom the process is indifferent,' as opposed to the conception of God, 'the Maker of Heaven and Earth,' and as opposed to mere 'Humanity,' 'the spirit of man, which is jealous, aggressive, and partisan,' who is the God whom, through centuries of unifying work towards a great future, man may come to know, in Chehov's words, 'by clear knowledge, as one knows that twice two are four.' In other words, God is the spirit in the world that, like transcendental imagination, contrives to make good use of opportunities offered by ever-changing nature.

It may seem strange that I should be dragging in Mr. Wells by the tail into a book which is supposed to deal with Chehov. It is because there is no modern Russian intellect who can hold a candle to Chehov, and because it has been asserted all too frequently that Chehov's attitude to life was pessimistic, 'hopeless,' 'gloomy,' and so forth. Neither Tolstoy's mentality nor Dostoevski's is really either modern or practical enough to serve as illustration (except by contrast) of Chehov's 'forward,' 'healthy' faith. And though habitually more preoccupied with individual men than with the destiny of man, Chehov shares another view with Mr. Wells—that unless we have a clear idea about the destiny of man, we must needs live futile lives among men ; that unless we bring the present into line with the future, we will live a life of futile misery and confusion in the present. Chehov has no such book as *The Undying Fire* to his credit, it is true. His thoughts on God and Man, etc., are squeezed in here and there, always with conspicuous moderation. But it may be said that in his ideas he anticipated Mr. Wells.

And now it may be asked what is Chehov's 'unifying' work towards that remote future 'when man will come to know the truth of the real God'? Well, it is his contribution to what he calls 'modern culture.' It is a great contribution in so far as his perfect impartiality, brought to bear upon the lives of individual men and women, reveals to us their differences and likenesses, the causes of their spiritual ills, and we perceive the common denominator of the human soul—the universal need for happiness. And we see, moreover, that its nature is conditional, that the conditions are easily adjustable; we see that, with a little intelligent exertion, so much misery and suffering need not have been. The reading of his tales invokes pity, sympathy, and understanding, not merely for human beings, but for all living creatures. For the rest, his contribution would depend on the degree in which his work invokes noble feelings in the reader.

His faith, as all genuine faith, was not immune from doubt. 'The "humane studies" of which you speak,' propounds the biologist Von Koren in *The Duel*, 'will only satisfy human thought when, as they advance, they meet the exact sciences and progress side by side with them.'

> Whether they will meet under a new microscope, or in the monologues of a new Hamlet, or in a new religion, I do not know, but I expect the earth will be covered with a crust of ice before it comes to pass.

This passage was written considerably earlier than the letter about that modern culture which is to culminate when man, in the remote future, comes to know the truth of the real God as clearly as a mathematical proposition. But the chronology of his professions of faith and doubt should not be taken to indicate any continuous development in him either in one direction or the other. The letter in which he declares his belief in the ultimate discovery of God by man, the God which in Mr. Wells's surmise may be as yet only foreshadowed in life, is, in its turn, succeeded by a letter to another friend, written two years later, and, in fact, four months before Chehov's death, which strikes a different note. '. . . All good wishes. Above all, be cheerful; don't look at life so much as a problem—it is, most likely, far simpler. And whether it—life, of which we know nothing—is worth all the agonising reflections which wear out our Russian wits is still a question.' Between scepticism and hope Chehov's conception of the world moodily fluctuates. And thus his art, too, fluctuates between his shrinking from the squalidness of everyday existence upward to the heavens, and his shrinking from the fatuities of sublimation downward upon earth. And in his note-book we find this, by way of a philosophical aside: 'But perhaps the universe is suspended on the tooth of some monster.'

At any rate, Chehov's contribution to 'modern culture' cannot be easily overlooked. If Mr. Wells is the driving force in the direction of salvation, the impatient traveller anxious to set out on the road, Chehov is the servant who packs his bags, turns out the room, anxious that nothing valuable be overlooked, anxious, too, that the traveller should not set out with too little luggage, lest he should have to come back for it again.

& VI

The convenience of comparing Chehov with Tolstoy is considerable; and the outstanding thing about Tolstoy, the driving force of him is that he was out to see the lie in life. Therefore he had direction and impetus, simplicity and penetration into human character. Tolstoy was a dynamic writer. He backed his conscience against everything else, and because of that there are few who would take it upon themselves to say that he was not a great man. But conscience can be a rather funny thing at times. Conscience, if you give way to it, may take the bit into its mouth and run away with you. Goodness was his goal, and when goodness is made a God of, goodness may be a little unkind. When we read Tolstoy we have a feeling as though we were listening to a passionate advocate exposing a system of evil in life which was highly abhorrent to ourselves. We applaud the advocate because we are hypnotised by his sincerity and ability. And it does not occur to us till long after his spell is broken that in his passionate desire to oust the lie he has perhaps seen a little more of it than there really is, that he has shown himself a little unjust towards the liars. But that this narrowness is the determining cause of his intensity is not always realized. When Turgenev wrote him his moving death-bed letter, in which he urged Tolstoy, '. . . my friend . . . great writer of the Russian Land,' to forsake his mental speculations and to return to his activity as a literary artist, he voiced the wishes of the majority of Tolstoy's admirers, but failed to understand that it was the sea of abstract truth that drew and caused, from the beginning, the onward rush of the big river, and that to deplore its having found its outlet to the open sea was to deplore the cause of a desirable effect, and that to ask

Tolstoy to become again a literary artist was to ask the river to change its course and flow backward against the current. Tolstoy was urged on by a purpose ; that purpose was truth; and that truth was of a quality contrary to everything he met in life. Truth made him see the lie in everything. And it is the clarity with which he saw the lie that made him a great artist.

With Chehov the position is reversed. With the same quick instinct he saw the lie, but he also saw farther and deeper. He saw the truth behind the lie. Life puzzled him, because, given to individualizing, he could always see the circumstantial inevitability of any sort of conduct; and the truth behind the lie evoked pity in him. And this is what made him a great artist. His keener and more delicate vision recognized that, in the words of his *Ivanov*, ' in each one of us there are too many springs, too many wheels and cogs for us to judge each other by first impressions or by two or three external indications.' Like the doctor that he was, and a keen psychologist into the bargain, he gives us his subtle diagnosis. But the remedy sometimes must be left to time. ' The explanation of this forgiveness of everything lies in my love for Sasha, but what is the explanation of this love itself, I really don't know.' Thus he concludes his story *Love*.

Tolstoy's heavy criticism of Chehov's *Darling* is characteristic of his different attitude to life. He supposed, innocently enough, that Chehov, like himself, was out to see the lie in life, and so must have wished to ' curse the modern woman ' when he wrote *The Darling*. From one unwarranted conclusion he jumps to another, and suggests that Chehov has ' blessed her ' instead ; and from that to a third, that Chehov has blessed her, in fact, by mistake, and so has written his beautiful tale as it were by a stroke of accident! But Chehov did not mind a bit. 'I hear Tolstoy is reading *The Darling* in an amusing fashion,' he tells his sister in a letter, evidently rather delighted at the news. But Tolstoy was moved profoundly by the story. 'I, at least,' he says in the same review, 'cannot read it without tears.'

And so Chehov paints all saints and sinners with an equally sympathetic brush. Instinctively, he steps into the shoes of every individual he portrays. 'You abuse me,' he writes in a letter to his friend Suvorin, 'for objectivity, calling it indifference to good and evil, lack of ideals and ideas, and so on. You would have me, when I describe horse-stealers, say: "Stealing horses is an evil." But that has been known for ages without my saying so. Let the jury judge them; it's my job simply to show what sort of people they are. I write: you are dealing with horse-stealers, so let me tell you that they are not beggars but well-fed people, that they are people of a special cult, and that horse-stealing is not simply theft but a passion.' It is the individual always that his humanity is concerned with, the suffering unit. And understanding all the motives, he sees the truth behind the lie—and there is no lie. The only lie would be to fail to understand.

CHAPTER THREE

THE DETERMINING CAUSES OF HIS SENSIBILITY; AND THE RELEVANT CIRCUMSTANCES OF HIS LIFE

§I

'How PLEASANT it is to respect people! When I see books, I am not concerned with how the authors loved or played cards; I see only their marvellous works.'

And perhaps it would be proper to treat his own life in the spirit of this fragment from his note-book, and to dwell only on those circumstances of his varied but scarcely dramatic life which are more relevant to his work. There is the other case, of course, that of legitimate curiosity about essentially irrelevant details of the life of a great writer, which should be reasonably satisfied. But Chehov is singularly lacking in that foppery which is perhaps traditionally cultivated by the less talented exponents of the arts, who persuade themselves thereby that they have the so-called 'artistic temperament.' And that painful public deference to his person and his work is completely lacking in him. No one could be more unlike Mr. George Moore, in this respect, than Chehov. Yet Chehov is an artist to his fingertips.

Nor was Chehov modest because he did not know his own worth. Far from it. Here is an extract from a letter to his friend Suvorin (the Russian Northcliffe), which bears testimony to the fact that Chehov was alive to his own powers:

You say that the hero of my *Party* is a character worth developing. Good Lord! I am not a senseless brute, you know.

I understand that I cut the throats of my characters and spoil them, and that I waste good material. . . . To tell you the truth, I would gladly have spent six months over *The Party*; I like taking things easy, and see no attraction in publishing at headlong speed. I would willingly, with pleasure, with feeling, in a leisurely way, describe the *whole* of my hero, describe the state of his mind while his wife was in labour, his trial, the horrid feeling he has after he is acquitted; I would describe the midwife and the doctors having tea in the middle of the night; I would describe the rain. . . . It would give me nothing but pleasure because I like to rummage about and dawdle. But what am I to do? I begin a story on September 10th with the thought that I must finish it by October 5th at the latest; if I don't I shall fail the editor and be left without money. I let myself go at the beginning and write with an easy mind; but by the time I get to the middle I begin to grow timid and to fear that my story will be too long: I have to remember that the *Severni Vestnik* has not much money, and that I am one of their expensive contributors. This is why the beginning of my stories is always very promising and looks as though I were starting on a novel, the middle is huddled and timid, and the end is, as in a short sketch, like fireworks. And so in planning a story one is bound to think first about its framework: from a crowd of main or subordinate characters one selects one person only—wife or husband; one puts him on the canvas and paints him alone, making him prominent, while the others one scatters over the canvas like small coin, and the result is something like the vault of heaven: one big moon and a number of very small stars around it. But the moon is not a success because it can only be understood if the stars too are intelligible, and the stars are not worked out. And so what I produce is not literature, but something like the patching of Trishka's coat. What am I to do? I don't know and I don't. I must trust to time, which heals all things.

Nor is he modest only for his knowledge that at this stage—when he was twenty-eight—he had not done as much as he could have done, given the leisure and financial independence. It was his sense of delicacy and his sense of the ridiculous which warned him not to be fastidious about his work in public. Modesty can be cultivated out of delicacy, from a sensitive consideration of the susceptibility of others. But for a swift survey of his career, and for a rapid indication of some of the determining causes of his sensibility, I cannot do better than give Chehov's own abridged autobiography, written in answer to a request, five years before his death:

Autobiography? I have a disease—autobiographobia. To read any sort of details about myself, and still more to write them for print, is a veritable torture to me. On a separate sheet I send a few facts, very bald, but I can do no more. . . .

I, A. P. Chehov, was born on the 17th of January, 1860, at Taganrog. I was educated first in the Greek School near the church of Tsar Constantine; then in the Taganrog high school. In 1879 I entered Moscow University in the Faculty of Medicine. I had at the time only a slight idea of the Faculties in general, and chose the Faculty of Medicine, I don't remember on what grounds, but did not regret my choice afterwards. I began in my first year to publish stories in the weekly journals and newspapers, and these literary pursuits had, early in the eighties, acquired a permanent professional character. In 1888 I took the Pushkin prize. In 1890 I travelled to the Island of Sakhalin, to write afterwards a book upon our penal colony and prisons there. Not counting reviews, feuilletons, paragraphs, and all that I have written from day to day for the newspapers, which it would be difficult now to seek out and collect, I have, during my twenty years of literary work, published more than three hundred signatures of print, or short and long stories. I have also written plays for the stage.

I have no doubt that the study of medicine has had an important influence on my literary work; it has considerably enlarged the sphere of my observation, has enriched me with knowledge the true value of which for me as a writer can only be understood by one who is himself a doctor. It has also had a guiding influence, and it is probably due to my close association with medicine that I have succeeded in avoiding many mistakes.

Familiarity with the natural sciences and with scientific methods has always kept me on my guard, and I have always tried, where it was possible, to be consistent with the facts of science, and where it was impossible I have preferred not to write at all. I may observe in passing that the conditions of artistic creation do not always admit of complete harmony with the facts of science. It is impossible to represent upon the stage a death from poisoning exactly as it takes place in reality. But harmony of the facts of science must be felt even under those conditions—i.e. it must be clear to the reader or spectator that this is only due to the conditions of art, and that he has to do with a writer who understands.

I do not belong to the class of literary men who take up a sceptical attitude towards science ; and to the class of those who rush into anything with only their own imagination to go upon, I should not like to belong.

Chehov's distinction as a writer of genius, out of a multitude of ordinary, kindly, and intelligent human beings, was simply that the proportion of the ordinary human gifts was in him perfect to an extraordinarily rare degree. Let me quote Trigorin's conversation with the admiring Nina in the *Sea-Gull*, in which Chehov's attitude to his literary life is well expressed. I do not pretend that Trigorin is the one and only personal sketch in all of Chehov's writing, for there are bits of Chehov in very many of his characters. But Trigorin is the completest picture of himself that the 'objective-minded' Chehov ever cared to paint, and, within limits, can be safely taken to be Chehov himself.

Violent obsessions sometimes lay hold of a man : he may, for instance, think day and night of nothing but the moon. I have such a moon. Day and night I am held in the grip of one besetting idea : I must write, I must write, I must... Hardly have I finished one story than for some reason I must write another, then a third, then a fourth. . . Why, What's there so lofty and beautiful about that, I ask you? Oh, what a wild life! Here I am, thrilled by your presence, but all the time I remember that an unfinished story awaits me. I see that cloud there, which resembles a piano. I reflect: I must mention somewhere in the story that a cloud was floating resembling a piano. It smells of heliotrope. I tell myself: a sickly smell, a colour worn by widows, mention when describing a summer evening. I try to catch myself and you at every phrase, at every word, and hasten to lock up these treasures in my literary store-room: in case they should come in useful! When I finish work I rush off to the theatre, or else go fishing; now it would seem was the time to rest, to forget yourself, but no! The heavy iron cannon ball is already rolling in my head—a new plot, and my table is calling me, and again I must hasten to write. And always so, and there's no rest for me from myself, and I feel I am eating my own life, that for the honey I give away to some one remote into space I brush the bloom from the best of my flowers, tear the very flowers and trample the roots.

The same Trigorin feels as though his relatives and friends did not treat him as a normal human being. 'What are you writing now? What will you give us next?' is the perpetual question. Their praise and attention seems somehow unreal and unnatural to him—as though he were a sick patient who was being carefully deceived about the real state of his health. Presently, he feels, they will come up to him gently from behind, take him by the shoulders to the waiting ambulance and convey him to the lunatic asylum. This is how he feels about his fame. He did not see his reader, but for some reason he imagined him to be unsympathetic and distrustful; and when his plays were being performed it always seemed to him that the dark-haired men were hostile and the blond ones coldly indifferent. Nina interrupts him to ask if the actual writing was not exhilarating, and Trigorin says: 'Yes. When I write it's agreeable. And reading the proof is agreeable, but . . . no sooner has it come out in print than I feel I can't endure it, and it's already plain to me that the whole thing's a mistake, that I shouldn't have written it. . . But the public comments: "Yes, charming, clever. . . Clever, but a long way off Tolstoy," or: "A beautiful thing, but Turgenev's *Fathers and Children* is better." And so to my dying day it will only be charming and clever, charming and clever, and when I die, my friends in passing by my grave will say: "Here lies Trigorin. He was a good writer, but he wrote worse than Turgenev."'

'Forgive me, but I fail to understand you,' rejoins his young admirer. 'You're simply spoiled by success.'

'What success? I never cared for myself. I don't care for myself as a writer. The worst of it all is, that I am in a kind of trance and often don't understand myself what I write. . . I love this water, these trees, the sky. I feel nature, she inspires in me a passion, an overwhelming desire, to write. But I am not merely a landscape painter, I am a citizen, too, I love my country, the people, I feel that if I am a writer I am bound to talk of the people, of their suffering, of their future, talk of science, of the right of man, and so on, and so on, and I speak of it all, I hurry, they drive me on from all sides, get angry, I dart from one side to another, like a fox with the hounds on his heels, I see that life and science are always advancing, while I am more and more losing ground, like a peasant who has just missed the train.'

& II

Chehov's name, by the way, had much better be spelt as I spell it. This is the nearest to both the Russian spelling and pronunciation. And transliteration from the Russian, as Mr. Aylmer Maude long ago observed, is a compromise between the two—due regard always given to the simplicity, shortness, and directness of the rendering. While living abroad, Chehov himself had made use of more than one transliteration of his name. But there is certainly no need whatever for the initial 'T,' so far as the English transliteration goes. However, this is not very important.

When one thinks of Chehov and then remembers that he was actually the grandson of a serf, indeed, strictly speaking, the son of an ex-serf, for it was his grandfather who purchased his own freedom and that of his family, one begins to realize the extraordinary homogeneity of the Russian people. One also realizes the incalculable possibilities of Russia's future, following upon the stimulus of a wider education.

Here is a piece of dialogue between the successful merchant whose father was an illiterate peasant, and Trofimov, the 'eternal student' (*The Cherry Orchard*):—

TROFIMOV. Don't wave your hands about! Get rid of that habit of waving them about... All the same, I like you. You've thin, delicate fingers [like Chehov himself], like those of an artist, and you've a sensitive, delicate soul.

LOPAHIN. . . . Well, as I was saying, I made forty thousand roubles, and I mean I'd like to lend you some, because I can afford it. Why turn up your nose at it? I'm just a simple peasant.

TROFIMOV. Your father was a peasant, mine was a chemist, and nothing whatever follows from it.

Anton Chehov's grandfather purchased his freedom and that of his family for 3,500 roubles (then about £350), with one daughter thrown in for nothing. Chehov's father started life as a serf, and a few years after his freedom had been purchased, settled at Taganrog and opened a wholesale grocer's shop. And certainly 'nothing whatever followed from this,' since Anton Chehov, the son of a serf, is the most subtle and delicately discriminating, and yet also the most level-headed and humorous of all Russian writers, as well as the most truly civilized of men.

His father could sing, read music at sight, and play the violin, and also made a hobby of painting ikons. His mother was the daughter of a cloth merchant of fairly good education, with whom she had travelled in Russia, before he too settled at Taganrog. There were six children, five of whom were boys, Anton being the third son, born on the 17th of January, 1860, at Taganrog, a port on the Black Sea. He used to say in later years: 'Our talents we got from our father, but our soul from our mother.'

'Write a story of how a young man, the son of a serf,' he writes in a letter to Suvorin, also of peasant origin, but at that time the proprietor of the largest Russian newspaper, the *Novoe Vremya*,

> who has served in a shop, sung in a choir, been at a high school and a university, who has been brought up to respect everyone of higher rank and position, to kiss priests' hands, to reverence other people's ideas, to be thankful for every morsel of bread, who has been many times whipped, who has trudged from one pupil to another without goloshes, who has been used to fighting, and tormenting animals, who has liked dining with his rich relations, and been hypocritical before God and men from the mere consciousness of his own insignificance—write how this young man squeezes the slave out of himself, drop by drop, and how waking one beautiful morning he feels that he has no longer a slave's blood in his veins but a real man's.

After a stretch of good fortune, his father's luck turned; the grocer's shop went from bad to worse, till he was compelled to close it down, his house being sold by auction. The family removed to Moscow, while Anton, then only sixteen, remained behind and eked out a meagre income by giving lessons and so paying for his education at the high school. At that time he was fond of going to the theatre and of flirting with the school-girls. Three years later he went up to the University of Moscow, and rejoining his people, he gradually superseded his father in becoming the main, and soon the sole, support of the household. While at the University he wrote short sketches and stories, and on taking a degree in medicine he began to practise as a doctor. 'You advise me not to hunt after two hares and not to think of medical work,' he writes to Suvorin from Moscow:

> I don't know why one shouldn't hunt two hares even in the literal sense... I feel more confident and more satisfied with myself when I reflect that I have two professions and not one. Medicine is my lawful wife, and literature my mistress. When I get tired of one I spend the night with the other.

At that time he was always short of money, and usually implored the editor to pay him in advance. But the editor of the humorous journal to which Chehov was contributing happened not to be very affluent himself, and could not always afford to comply with Chehov's tragi-comical requests.

At the age of twenty-six he had occasion to reprimand a desultory brother who, because he was a painter, somehow thought that 'wine and women' were properly his equipment. The letter deals with specific failings, but also throws a light on Chehov's character. Here are some of the conditions which cultured people, in his view, must satisfy:

> 1. They respect human personality, and therefore they are always kind, gentle, polite, and ready to give in to others. They do not make a row because of a hammer or a lost piece of india-rubber; if they live with anyone, they do not regard it as a

favour, and, going away, they do not say, 'Nobody can live with you.' They forgive noise and cold and dried-up meat and witticisms and the presence of strangers in their homes.

2. They have sympathy not for beggars and cats alone. Their heart aches for what the eye does not see. . . . They sit up at night in order to help P. . . . to pay for brothers at the University, and to buy clothes for their mother.

3. They respect the property of others, and therefore pay their debts.

4. They are sincere, and dread lying like fire. They don't lie even in small things. A lie is insulting to the listener and puts him in a lower position in the eyes of the speaker. They do not pose, they behave in the street as they do at home, they do not show off before their humbler comrades. They are not given to babbling and forcing their uninvited confidences on others. Out of respect for other people's ears they more often keep silent than talk.

5. They do not disparage themselves to rouse compassion. They do not play on the strings of other people's hearts so that they may sigh and make much of them. They do not say, 'I am misunderstood,' or, 'I have become second-rate,' because all this is striving after cheap effect, is vulgar, stale, false. . .

6. They have no shallow vanity. They do not care for such false diamonds as knowing celebrities, shaking hands with the drunken P., listening to the raptures of a stray spectator in a picture show, being renowned in the taverns. If they do a pennyworth they do not strut about as though they had done a hundred roubles' worth, and do not brag of having the entry where others are not admitted. The truly talented always keep in obscurity among the crowd, as far as possible from advertisement. Even Krilov has said that an empty barrel echoes more loudly than a full one.

7. If they have a talent they respect it. They sacrifice to it rest, women, wine, vanity. They are proud of their talent. Besides, they are fastidious.

It is rather remarkable that there are no very definite periods in Chehov's development upon which one could fasten with advantage. For a long time his interests were about equally divided between medicine and literature, but it may be said that his real literary activity dates back from the year 1886, when he received, being then twenty-six, a generous letter of encouragement from the then famous veteran writer, Grigorovich. In reply, Chehov explains :

I felt that I had a gift, but I had got into the habit of thinking that it was insignificant. Purely external causes are sufficient to make one unjust to oneself, suspicious, and morbidly sensitive. And as I realize now, I have always had plenty of such causes. All my friends and relatives have always taken a condescending tone to my writing, and never ceased urging me in a friendly way not to give up real work for the sake of scribbling. . . In the course of the five years that I have been knocking about from one newspaper office to another, I have had time to assimilate the general view of my literary insignificance. I soon got used to looking down upon my work, and so it has gone from bad to worse. That is the first reason. The second is that I am a doctor, and am up to my ears in medical work, so that the proverb about trying to catch two hares has given to no one more sleepless nights than to me. [In spite of what he wrote to Suvorin !]

. . . Hitherto my attitude to my literary work has been frivolous, heedless, casual. I don't remember a *single* story over which I have spent more than twenty-four hours, and 'The Huntsman,' which you liked, I wrote in a bathing-shed ! I wrote my stories as reporters write their notes about fires, mechanically, half-unconsciously, taking no thought of the reader or myself. . . I wrote and did all I could not to waste upon the story the scenes and images dear to me which—God knows why—I have treasured and kept carefully hidden.

The first impulse to self-criticism was given me by a very kind and, to the best of my belief, sincere letter from Suvorin. I began to think of writing something decent, but I still had no faith in my being any good as a writer. And then, unexpected and undreamed of, came your letter. Forgive the comparison : it had on me the effect of a Governor's order to clear out of the town within twenty-four hours—i.e. I suddenly felt an imperative need to hurry, to make haste and get out of where I have stuck...

. . . I give to literature my spare time, two or three hours a day and a bit of the night, that is, time which is of no use except for short things. In the summer, when I have more time and fewer expenses, I will start on some serious work.

. . . I rest all my hopes on the future. I am only twenty-six. Perhaps I shall succeed in doing something, though time flies fast.

His subsequent meeting with Grigorovich in Petersburg, where the invalid writer lived, though pathetic was yet not without humour. The old man was so overcome with emotion at seeing his protégé that, in the act of embracing him, he had a heart-attack, and for several hours at a stretch Chehov, the doctor-author, attended at his host's bedside.

Apart from 1886, when, thanks to the encouragement received from Grigorovich, Chehov began to develop his own peculiar genius, there are no stages of development to speak of. The several periods to which Chehov's younger brother, Michael, refers in his biographical sketch, are really determined by Chehov's health and consequent changes of residence rather than by his intellectual development. All that can be usefully said is that as the years advanced, so his genius ground finer. This gradual development, if one is bound to look for landmarks, is best seen in the gradual improvement of his five four-act plays. The *Sea-Gull*, written in 1894, is better than *Ivanov*, written in 1887; *Uncle Vanya*, which was first produced in 1899 (and is a remodelled version of a hastily written play of 1889, then called the *Wood-Demon*), is better than the *Sea-Gull*; and *Three Sisters*, written in 1900, is better than *Uncle Vanya*, and as good as the *Cherry Orchard*, written in 1903, the year before Chehov's death, and commonly regarded as his masterpiece. His stories, all of which are dated in the Russian edition, fall into the periods, as it were, created by the plays, and are subject to the same advance in subtlety and maturity.

At the age of twenty-eight, after having written his first play, *Ivanov*, he confesses in a letter to Suvorin :

As far as my design goes, I was on the right track, but the execution is good for nothing. I ought to have waited! I am glad I did not listen to Grigorovich two or three years ago, and write a novel! I can just imagine what a lot of good material I should have spoilt. He says : ' Talent and freshness overcome everything.' It is more true to say that talent and freshness can spoil a great deal. In addition to plenty of material and talent, one wants something else which is no less important. One wants to be mature—that is one thing ; and for another the *feeling of personal freedom* is essential, and that feeling has only recently begun to develop in me. I used not to have it before ; its place was successfully filled by my frivolity, carelessness, and lack of respect for my work. What writers belonging to the upper class have received from nature for nothing, plebeians acquire at the cost of their youth.

The production of his first long play, *Ivanov*, at the age of twenty-nine, was important for him. It brought him into prominence. In it he attempted to say the last word on the subject of the traditional Russian hero harping the traditional Russian melody—disillusionment of life. He wanted to say it deliberately and objectively, because he held that hitherto the subject had been treated by writers unconsciously and subjectively, without any indication of the causes of the malady. The theme, the embryo of Chehov's sensibility, a novel and ambitious theme, for the theatre of all places, is an insistence that there are in human conduct fine shades and subtleties elusive of definition which defy the hard and fast and characteristically legal way of reasoning. In the play he gets several of the characters to put two and two together and make four; but the sum is wrong nevertheless, because they were wrong in putting two and two together from the start: in their credulity the judges of their fellows had overlooked the fractions which upset such simple calculations.

About this time he writes:

> They invite me everywhere and regale me with food and drink like a general at a wedding. My sister is indignant that people on all sides invite her simply because she is a writer's sister. No one wants to love the ordinary people in us.

Chehov's life henceforth resolves itself into developing the strip of land that he had purchased for himself and his family (comprising his father, mother, sister, aunt, and younger brother, all of whom he supported on his meagre earnings as a writer and a doctor), doctoring the peasants free of charge, building schools for them at his own expense, which he could ill afford to do, often borrowing money and working against time and health in order to repay it, the while slowly dying of consumption. We read of him now organizing famine relief in the stricken area, now setting off, almost single-handed, to combat the cholera epidemic in the district, now actively engaged in taking the census of the province. For the rest, he took occasional trips to Moscow, Petersburg, and abroad. On one occasion he took a journey across Siberia, returning by way of Vladivostok, Hong-Kong, Singapore and the Red Sea. On his return he wrote a book on the penal system, which, we are told, had a favourable effect on the authorities, and may have been one of the causes of the reforms that followed. Like all great men, he was keenly aware of the futility of punishment, but it must be remembered that in the Russia of his day he could not be too careful of what he said. And Chehov, it must be owned, was careful, and never had any trouble with the Russian Government. (Only one work of his was suppressed by the censor—a one-act play, entitled *On the Highway*, which is a little masterpiece. It was published after Chehov's death.) The fact that he avoided trouble was due to a quite proper feeling of self-preservation. The kind of heroism necessary to defy a Russian imperial government was about as sensible as the heroism necessary for, let us say, jumping out of the window. It was suicide, and, for a literary genius, unforgivable folly. Tolstoy alone, owing to his great reputation throughout the world, was moderately safe in speaking his mind. 'We are restrained,' Chehov writes to a friend, 'by an instinct of self-preservation and we are afraid.'

We are afraid of being overheard by some uncultured Esquimau who does not like us, and whom we don't like either. I personally am afraid that my acquaintance, N., whose cleverness attracts us, will hold forth with raised finger in every railway carriage and every house about me, settling the question why I became so intimate with X. while I was beloved by Z.

Politically, Chehov was—how shall I put it?—a reasonable man. This is what he writes to Suvorin on the subject of the student riots in 1899:

Chase nature out of the door, and she will fly in through the window; when there is no right to express one's opinions freely, then one expresses them provokingly, with aggravation and often, from the standpoint of the state, in an ugly and disgusting fashion. Give them freedom of the press and freedom of conscience, and then the desired tranquillity will set in, which, true enough, would not last very long, but would last our time, anyhow.

Something in the nature of a forecast of the Russian Revolution is to be found among the papers discovered in a special file entitled *Themes, Thoughts, Notes, and Fragments*, after his death:

I was irritated by smooth words and by those who speak them, and on reaching home I meditated thus: some rail at the world, others at the crowd, others again praise the past and blame the present; they cry out that there are no ideals, and so on, but all this was already going on twenty or thirty years ago; these are worn-out forms which have already served their time, and whoever repeats them now, he too is no longer young and is himself worn out. With last year's foliage there decay, too, those who live in it. It seemed to me that we uncultured, worn-out people, banal in speech, stereotyped in intention, have grown quite mouldy, and, while we intellectuals are rummaging among old rags and, according to the old Russian custom, biting one another, there is boiling up around us a life which we neither know nor notice. Great events will take us unawares, like sleeping fairies, and you will see that Sidorov, the merchant, and the teacher of the district school at Yeletz, who see and know more than we do, will push us far into the background, because they will have accomplished more than all of us together. And I thought that, were we now to obtain political liberty, of which we talk so much, while engaged in biting one another, we should not know what to do with it, we should waste it in accusing one another in the newspapers of being spies and money-grubbers, we should frighten society with the assurance that we have neither men, nor science, nor literature, nothing! Nothing! And to scare society as we are doing now, and as we shall continue to do, means to deprive it of courage; it means simply to declare that we have no social or political sense in us. And I also thought that, before the dawn of a new life has broken, we shall turn into sinister old men and women, and we shall be the first who, in our hatred of that dawn, will calumniate it.

And in a letter to a friend, he comments on the Russian intelligentsia:

I don't believe in our intelligentsia, which is hypocritical, false, hysterical, badly brought up, and lazy; I don't believe in her even when she's suffering and complaining, for her oppressors come from her own entrails. I believe in individual people, I see salvation in individual personalities scattered here and there all over Russia—whether they belong to the intelligentsia or to the peasants—they have strength though they are few.

On the subject of legal justice he writes in a letter:

Whether from our point of view the jury are mistaken or not mistaken, we ought to recognize that in each individual case they form a conscious judgment and make an effort to do so conscientiously; and if a captain steers his steamer conscientiously, continually consulting the chart and the compass, and if the steamer is nevertheless shipwrecked, would it not be more correct to put down the shipwreck, not to the captain, but to something else—for instance, to think that the chart is out of date or that the bottom of the sea has changed?... Apart from the criminal law, the penal code, and legal procedure, there is a moral law, which is always in advance of the established law, and which defines our actions precisely when we try to act on our conscience... In the same way it sometimes happens to the jury to be put in a position in which they feel that their conscience is not satisfied by the established law, that in the case they are judging there are fine shades and subtleties which cannot be brought under the provisions of the penal code, and that obviously something else is needed for a just judgment, and that for the lack of that 'something' they will be forced to give a judgment in which something is lacking.

In a letter to Suvorin concerning the famous Dreyfus case, then agitating the public mind, among other things he says:

Let Dreyfus be guilty, and Zola is still right, since it is the duty of writers, not to accuse, not to prosecute, but to champion even the guilty once they have been condemned and are enduring punishment. I shall be told: 'What of the political position, the interests of the State?' But great writers and artists ought to take part in politics only so far as they have to protect themselves from politics. There are plenty of accusers, prosecutors, and gendarmes without them, and, in any case, the rôle of Paul suits them better than that of Saul.

❧ III

In his letters to his friends Chehov constantly insists that it is the writer's business to act in the capacity of judge, merely putting the right questions, and leaving the answers to the reader, who constitutes the jury. 'You confuse two things,' he writes to Suvorin, '*solving* a problem and *stating* a problem *correctly*. It is only the second that is obligatory for the artist. In *Anna Karenina* and *Evgeni Onegin* not a single problem is solved, but they satisfy you completely because all the problems are correctly stated in them.'

The writer, Chehov says, is as necessary 'as a star is to an astronomer.' 'We have specialists for dealing with special questions: it is their business to judge of the commune, of the future of capitalism, of the evils of drunkenness, of boots, of the diseases of women,' he writes in a letter. These specialists are the people, the astronomers, so to speak, who can make use of him as he reflects life for them. He is the star that they may trust as they make their calculations. And here he hits upon his proper place in modern civilization. He corroborates his view:

That in his [the literary artist's] sphere there are no questions, but only answers, can be maintained only by those who have never written and have had no experience of thinking in images. An artist observes, selects, guesses, combines—and this in itself presupposes a question: unless he had set himself a question from the very first, there would be nothing to conjecture and nothing to select. To put it briefly, I will end by using the language of psychiatry: if one denies that creative work involves problems and purposes, one must admit that an artist creates without premeditation or intention, in a state of aberration; therefore, if an author boasted to me of having written a novel without a preconceived design, under a sudden inspiration, I should call him mad.

He is certainly not an 'Art for Art's Saker.' Art for art's sake is to him like eating for its own sake—a nonsensical proposition. 'Sienkiewicz has evidently not read Tolstoy,' he writes, 'and does not know Nietzsche':

he talks about hypnotism like a shopman; on the other hand, every page is positively sprinkled with Rubens, Borghesi, Correggio, Botticelli—and that is done to show off his culture to the bourgeois reader and make a long nose on the sly at materialism. The object of the novel is to lull the bourgeoisie to sleep in its golden dreams. Be faithful to your wife, pray with her over the prayer-book, save money, love sport, and all is well with you in this world and the next. The bourgeoisie is very fond of so-called practical types and novels with happy endings, since they soothe it with the idea that one can both accumulate capital and preserve innocence, be a beast and at the same time be happy.

His attitude to criticism is interesting. He wanted critics, he deplored their absence. 'Literary society,' he writes, 'students, Pleshcheyev [a veteran poet], young ladies, etc., were enthusiastic in their praises of my "Nervous Breakdown," but Grigorovich was the only one who noticed the description of the first snow.'

If we had critics, I should know that I provide material, whether good or bad does not matter—that to men who devote themselves to the study of life I am as necessary as a star is to an astronomer. . . A number of tribes, religions, languages, civilizations, have vanished without a trace—vanished because there were no historians or biologists. In the same way a number of lives and works of art disappear before our very eyes owing to the complete absence of criticism. It may be objected that critics would have nothing to do because all modern works are poor and insignificant. But this is a narrow way of looking at things. Life must be studied not from the pluses alone, but from the minuses too. The conviction that the 'eighties' have not produced a single writer may in itself provide material for five volumes.

He was dissatisfied with Merezhkovski's magazine article about him. Merezhkovski, in Chehov's view, 'writes smoothly and youthfully, but at every page loses heart, makes reservations and concessions, and this means that he is not clear upon the subject.' And Chehov gradually begins to doubt whether critics really know anything that he does not know himself. He writes:

When people talk to me of what is artistic and inartistic, of what is dramatic and not dramatic, of tendency, realism, and so on, I am bewildered, hesitatingly assent, and answer with banal half-truths not worth a brass farthing. I divide all works into two classes: those I like and those I don't. I have no other criterion, and if you ask me why I like Shakespeare and don't like Zlatovratski [a third-rate writer], I don't venture to answer. Perhaps in time, and as I grow wiser, I may work out some criterion, but meanwhile all conversations about what is 'artistic' only weary me, and seem to me like a continuation of the scholastic disputations with which people wearied themselves in the Middle Ages. If criticism, on the authority of which you rely, knows what you and I don't know, why has it up till now not spoken? why does it not reveal the truth and the immutable laws? ... If it knew, believe me, it would long ago have shown us the true path... But criticism maintains a dignified silence or gets out of it with trashy babble. If it seems to you authoritative, it is because it is stupid, conceited, impudent, and clamorous; because it is an empty barrel one cannot help hearing.

Years later, in a letter to Vladimir Nemirovich-Danchenko, the founder of the Moscow Art Theatre, which had made its reputation chiefly over Chehov's plays, he writes concerning a review of *Uncle Vanya,* in which the people of his play were compared with types from Goncharov and Turgenev:

It is repulsive to me—this yoking up to 'Oblomov,' to 'Fathers and Children.' You can yoke up any play to whatever you please, and if Sanin and Ignatiev [the reviewers] had taken Nozdrëv instead of Oblomov, or King Lear, it would have come out equally profound and readable. I do not read such articles in order not to choke up my mood with rubbish.

Again, to Suvorin:

I should read now with pleasure, even with joy, something serious, not merely about myself, but things in general. I pine for serious reading, and recent Russian criticism does not nourish, but simply irritates me. I could read with enthusiasm something new about Pushkin or Tolstoy. That would be balsam for my idle mind.

And yet again:

I send you Mihailovski's article on Tolstoy. Read it and grow perfect. It's a good article, but it's strange: one might write a thousand such articles and things would not be one step forwarder, and it would still remain unintelligible why such articles are written.

Here is a relevant extract from his note-book:

A professor's opinion: not Shakespeare, but the commentaries on him are the thing.

And to wind up with the subject of criticism, Maxim Gorki tells us in his *Reminiscences of Chehov* what Chehov said to him on the subject of critics:

'Critics are like horse-flies which prevent the horse from ploughing,' he said, smiling his wise smile. 'The horse works, all its muscles drawn tight like the strings on a double-bass, and a fly settles on his flanks and tickles and buzzes . . . he has to twitch his skin and swish his tail. And what does the fly buzz about? It scarcely knows itself; simply because it is restless and wants to proclaim: "Look, I too am living on the earth. See, I can buzz too, buzz about anything." For twenty-five years I have read criticisms of my stories, and I don't remember a single remark of any value or one word of valuable advice. Only once Skabichevski wrote something which made an impression on me . . . he said I would die in a ditch, drunk.'

In the *Sea-Gull*, the wily actress thus praises her lover, the fashionable writer Trigorin; and what she says to him applies in fact to Chehov himself, and I think there can be little doubt that while writing it Chehov must have realized this:

You are so talented, so wise, the best of all living writers. . . You have so much sincerity, simplicity, freshness, sound humour. . . You can, by a single stroke, convey the essential, that which is typical of a character or of a landscape, your people are like living people. Oh, one cannot read you without rapture.

Perhaps he has said here what the critics had all along failed to say about his work.

& IV

Much can be gathered from his opinions of Tolstoy, Turgenev, Gogol, Goncharov. 'I am cold in my barn,' he writes to Suvorin. 'I should like new carpets, an open fireplace, bronzes, and learned conversations. Alas! I shall never be a Tolstoyan. In women I love beauty above all things; and in the history of mankind, culture, expressed in carpets, spring carriages, and keenness of wit. *Ach!* to make haste and become an old man and sit at a big table!. . .' One wonders whether Chehov was not drawn to bronzes and carpets and spring carriages partly because of their comparative novelty to him; and whether Tolstoy's craving for a life *à la* Jean-Jacques was not because he had had too much of the other thing from his birth. Were they not both reacting from what had wearied them? 'Perhaps because I am not smoking,' Chehov writes, 'Tolstoy's morality has ceased to touch me; at the bottom of my heart I take up a hostile attitude towards it, and that, of course, is not just.'

I have peasant blood in my veins, and you won't astonish me with peasant virtues. From my childhood I have believed in progress, and I could not help believing in it since the difference between the time when I used to be thrashed and when they gave up thrashing me was tremendous. . . But Tolstoy's philosophy touched me profoundly and took possession of me for six or seven years, and what affected me was not its general propositions, with which I was familiar beforehand, but Tolstoy's manner of expressing it, his reasonableness, and probably a sort of hypnotism. Now something in me protests, reason and justice tell me that in the electricity and heat of love for man there is something greater than chastity and abstinence from meat. War is an evil and legal justice is an evil; but it does not follow from that that I ought to wear bark shoes and sleep on the stove with the labourer, and so on, and so on. But that is not the point, it is not a matter of *pro* and *con*; the thing is that in one way or another Tolstoy has passed for me, he is not in my soul, and he has departed from me, saying: 'I leave this your house empty.' I am untenanted. I am sick, of theorizing of all sorts, and such bounders as Max Nordau I read with positive disgust. Patients in a fever do not want food, but they do want something, and that vague craving they express as 'longing for something sour.' I, too, want something sour, and that's not a mere chance feeling, for I notice the same mood in others around me. It is just as if they had all been in love, had fallen out of love, and now were looking for some new distraction.

Again:

Tolstoy is writing a little book about Art. He came to see me in the clinic, and said that he had flung aside his novel 'Resurrection' as he did not like it, and was writing only about Art, and had read sixty books about Art. His idea is not a new one, all intelligent old men in all the ages have sung the same tune in different keys. Old men have always been prone to see the end of the world, and have always declared that morality was degenerating to the uttermost point, that Art was growing feeble, and so on, and so on. Lev Nikolaievich wants to persuade us in his little book that at the present time Art has entered upon its final phase, that it is in a blind alley, from which it has no outlet (except retreat).

. . . That's just like saying the desire to eat and drink has grown old, has outlived its day, and is not what it ought to be. Of course, hunger is an old story. In the desire to eat we have got into a blind alley; but still, eating is necessary, and we shall go on eating, however the philosophers and irate old men moralize.

But nevertheless his respect for his great contemporary remained unadulterated. 'Tolstoy! ah, Tolstoy!' he writes in regard to the efforts of the novelist to alleviate the famine. 'In these days he is not a man, but a super-man, a Jupiter. In the *Sbornik* he has published an article about the relief centres, and the article consists of advice and practical instructions. So business-like, simple, and sensible.'

And again:

His [Tolstoy's] illness frightened me, and kept me on tenterhooks. I am afraid of Tolstoy's death. If he were to die, there would be a big empty place in my life. To begin with, because I have never loved any man as much as him. I am not a believing man, but of all beliefs I consider his the nearest and most akin to me. Secondly, while Tolstoy is in literature it is easy and pleasant to be a literary man; even recognizing that one has done nothing, and never will do anything, it is not so dreadful, since Tolstoy will do enough for all. His work is the justification of the enthusiasm and expectations built upon literature. Thirdly, Tolstoy takes a firm stand, he has an immense authority, and so long as he is alive, bad tastes in literature, vulgarity of every kind, insolent and lachrymose, all the bristling, exasperated vanities will be in the far background, in the shade. Nothing but his moral authority is capable of maintaining a certain elevation in the moods and tendencies of literature so called. Without him they would be a flock without a shepherd, or a hotch-potch, in which it would be difficult to discriminate anything.

'. . . Tolstoy came to see me; we talked of immortality,' is an entry in his diary.

Gorki, in his *Reminiscences of Tolstoy*, writes:

He loved Chehov, and when he looked at him, his eyes were tender and seemed almost to stroke Anton Pavlovich's face. Once, when Anton Pavlovich was walking on the lawn with Alexandra Lvovna [Tolstoy's daughter], Tolstoy, who at the time was still ill and was sitting in a chair on the terrace, seemed to stretch towards them, saying in a whisper: 'Ah, what a beautiful, magnificent man: modest and quiet like a girl! And he walks like a girl. He's simply wonderful.'

'I know Tolstoy,' writes Chehov in a letter to a friend, 'it seems to me that I know him well, and I understand every movement of his brows, but still I love him.' And again: 'I have seen Tolstoy. Wise, wise eyes...'

There is perhaps nothing more fascinating than to read of the attitude of one great writer to another. Mr. Aylmer Maude, in his impressive volumes on Tolstoy's life, has a chapter on the quarrel between Tolstoy and Turgenev. He tells it with an engaging impartiality, and the situation, by virtue of the earnestness with which the two great novelists intended to blow each other's brains out, is not without humour. In fact, the quarrel from beginning to end is extremely funny. The funniest part of it, though, was when Turgenev, after the reconciliation, visited Tolstoy and sought to be humorous at dinner and amuse the latter's children by imitating various animals, while Tolstoy refused to be intimidated or to see anything funny in Turgenev's antics. Temperamentally, compared with Chehov, both Turgenev and Tolstoy seem children in their sudden ineffective angers, in their ridiculous challenges. One learns that Turgenev dissuaded Dostoevski from making the acquaintance of the author of *War and Peace*, warning him that Tolstoy's temper was impossible. I would give much to know what Turgenev would have thought of Chehov's works had he been spared to live to read them. Tolstoy's opinion of his novels, while Turgenev lived, was not a very high one ; but in the sentimental mood that came upon him after the death of his contemporary he professed to be profoundly touched by them, as he re-read them in preparation for a lecture on the dead Turgenev, which, however—a characteristically Russian phenomenon !—was forbidden by the police. Tolstoy's attitude to Dostoevski, Gorki tells us, was not over-generous, though it was shrewd: he said that Dostoevski had a peculiarly suspicious, restless mind, and that his characters were psychological inventions, that there were no such people in Russia or elsewhere. 'I bought Dostoevski in your shop,' Chehov writes to Suvorin, 'and am now reading him. It is fine, but very long and indiscreet. It is over-pretentious.'

Of Gorki Chehov writes : 'By appearance he is a tramp,

but inwardly this is rather an elegant man. . . I want to introduce him to women, as I find this useful for him, but he is trying to back out of it.'

'Among other things I am reading Goncharov,' Chehov writes in a letter to Suvorin, 'and wondering.'

I wonder how I could have considered Goncharov a first-rate writer. His 'Oblomov' is not really good. Oblomov himself is exaggerated and is not so striking as to make it worth while to write a whole book about him. The other characters are trivial, with a flavour of Leikin about them; they are taken at random, and are half unreal. . . And the chief trouble is that the whole novel is cold, cold, cold. I cross out Goncharov from the list of my demi-gods.

'But,' he writes, 'how direct, how powerful is Gogol, and what an artist he is! His "Marriage" alone is worth two hundred thousand roubles. It is simply delicious, and that is all about it. He is the greatest of Russian writers. In "The Inspector-General" the first act is the best, in "Marriage" the third act is the worst. I am going to read it aloud to my people.'

Of Turgenev he writes:

My God! What a glorious thing 'Fathers and Children' is! It is positively terrifying. Bazarov's illness is so powerfully done that I felt ill and had a sensation as though I had caught the infection from him. And the end of Bazarov? And the old men? And Kukshina? It's—it's beyond words. It's simply a work of genius. I don't like the whole of 'On the Eve,' only Elena's father and the end. The end is full of tragedy. 'The Dog' is very good, the language is wonderful in it. Please read it if you have forgotten it. 'Acia' is charming, 'A Quiet Backwater' is too compressed and not satisfactory. I don't like 'Smoke' at all. 'The House of Gentlefolk' is weaker than 'Fathers and Children,' but the end is like a miracle, too. Except for the old woman in 'Fathers and Children'—that is, Bazarov's mother—and the mothers as a rule, especially the society women, who are, however, all alike (Liza's mother, Elena's mother), and Lavretski's mother, who had been a serf, and the humble peasant women, all Turgenev's girls and women are insufferable in their artificiality, and—forgive my saying it—falsity. Liza and Elena are not Russian girls, but some sort of Pythian prophetesses, full of extravagant pretensions. Irina in 'Smoke,' Madame Odintsov in 'Fathers and Children,' all the lionesses, in fact, fiery, alluring, insatiable creatures, for ever craving for something, are all nonsensical. When one thinks of Tolstoy's 'Anna Karenina,' all these young ladies of Turgenev's, with their seductive shoulders, fade away into nothing. The negative types of women where Turgenev is slightly caricaturing (Kukshina) or jesting (the description of balls) are wonderfully drawn, and so successful that, as the saying is, you can't pick a hole in it.

One recalls the picture of Tolstoy and Chehov on the latter's visit to Yasnaya Polyana: the aristocratic novelist, author of the longest novel in the world, almost deliberately uncouth in his comfortable peasant garb, and the greatest modern dramatist and writer of short-stories, dressed in an ordinary lounge-suit, wearing a pince-nez on a black cord, tall, slight, strikingly good-looking, and a little timid, sitting gingerly at the side of his renowned contemporary on an uncomfortable garden chair. It has become the habit in some quarters to deride Tolstoy for his attire on the ground that it was an affectation. This is unjust. For it was more comfortable for Tolstoy to dress in the Russian country manner, since he lived in the country. Nor can the æsthetic advantage of the 'great writer of the Russian land,' as Turgenev on his death-bed called him, attired in a simple Russian blouse, be overlooked, all the more so when you remember that Tolstoy's somewhat coarse, ungainly face was conspicuously out of place in a European costume. The bare feet, as seen on the famous Repin picture, are, of course, the painter's own addition.

'I have given him food and drink,' was Tolstoy's laughing comment on Repin's picture, 'and he's taken my boots from me.' One fancies that Tolstoy must have done most of the talking, no doubt with that ponderous simplicity that goes down so well in Russian, but which is so hopelessly threadbare when translated into any Western tongue. Tolstoy's questions, we gather from Gorki, were intentionally direct, and just a little naïve in so far as he seemed unaware that some of his hearers were aware of it. But all his utterances were received with awe, and Chehov actually confessed to Gorki that it was a matter of regret that every utterance of the great Tolstoy was not being taken down assiduously, as in the case of Goethe. Tolstoy loved Chehov, but there was a touch of patronizing tenderness in his attitude to the younger man. Not that Chehov in the least resented it. But I think it will be admitted that Tolstoy, by virtue of the commanding intellectual position in which his dynamic genius placed him, was apt to be at times a little trying, and intolerant, and unjust, and even a little clumsy. One day, as he saw Chehov out, he said to him good-naturedly, much to Chehov's amusement: 'You are a very good fellow, and I am very fond of you; and, as you know, I can't bear Shakespeare, but still, his plays are better than yours!' Tolstoy was 'interested' in Chehov's plays; but that seems to have been all. Though it may very likely be that Tolstoy's failure to appreciate their disturbing beauty, their dramatic daring, may be accounted for by the fact that the last two plays, *Three Sisters* and the *Cherry Orchard*, had not yet been written. For there is no excuse for failing to appreciate them. Tolstoy thought highly of Chehov as a writer of short-stories, calling him the Russian Maupassant; but regretted that his works expressed no clear philosophy of conduct, and said that Chehov would have been an even better writer but for his medical training. The comparison with Maupassant is a little naïve. One could understand Maupassant being called the French Chehov, in a mood of generous extravagance. But it was well meant; and, after all, Maupassant preceded Chehov, and both of them excelled in the short-story; nor do we know how much Chehov had accomplished when Tolstoy conferred the compliment upon him.

Chehov had a keener and more delicate sense of humour than Tolstoy: he could afford to laugh at himself more easily—a gift which in Tolstoy, because of his burning sense of shame for the ignoble (his acute conscience, which, it will be remembered, he said was the only sign of God in man), was often checked, and totally extinguished when he undertook that last railway journey, so unnecessarily theatrical, since he himself abhorred theatricality—no man more.

& V

Chehov was fond of saying that a writer has no need of note-books, since his memory ought to be his note-book. But when he died, it was discovered that his writing-table drawer was full of note-books.

In a letter from Nice, where he was compelled to spend the winter on more than one occasion, he confesses to a friend that he had noticed that, by a curious coincidence, whenever he wrote much he was invariably poor, and incidentally, whenever he felt gay he wrote dreary stories, and *vice versa*. *Ward No.* 6 was written while he was in the best of spirits. But Chehov himself did not favour it, 'owing to a complete absence of woman and the element of love.' 'I can't endure such stories,' he writes. 'I write them, as it were, by accident, thoughtlessly.' While abroad, he spared no pains in sending books to the new municipal library of his native Taganrog, which he equipped with complete editions of the Western classics. The library is dedicated to his memory.

In the latter part of his life Chehov was compelled to live more or less permanently in the Crimea. His health was ruined, his lungs could not hold out in the northern climate which he loved. He was consequently obliged to sell the estate at Melihovo, into which he had put so much work. At that time he sold the complete collection of his works, as well as those to come, to a Petersburg publisher, and he was able to buy some land at Yalta and build a house; and it was here that in the autumn of 1900 he wrote the *Three Sisters*. 'Oh, do not tire, do not grow cold!' he writes to his friend Nemirovich-Danchenko, the founder of the Art Theatre at Moscow. 'The Art Theatre is the best pages of that book which one day will be written about the contemporary Russian theatre. That theatre is your pride, and it is the only theatre which I love, though I have never been in it. If I lived in Moscow, I would try to join your staff, if only as a porter, to prevent your growing cold towards that charming institution.' In the same letter, dated November, 1899, he says that he has a plot for a new play—*Three Sisters*. In the same year *Uncle Vanya* was being played at Moscow, with considerable success. This is what Chehov writes to Olga Knipper, an actress of the Art Theatre, whom he married two years later:

You ask me whether I shall be excited, but you see I only heard properly that 'Uncle Vanya' was to be given on the twenty-sixth from your letter, which I got on the twenty-seventh. The telegrams began coming on the evening of the twenty-seventh, when I was in bed. They send them on to me by telephone. I woke up every time and ran with bare feet to the telephone, and got very much chilled ; then I had scarcely dozed off when the bell rang again and again. It's the first time that my own fame has kept me awake. The next evening when I went to bed I put my slippers and dressing-gown beside my bed, but there were no more telegrams.

We are told that when the *Three Sisters* was performed for the first time at the Art Theatre in Moscow it made a deep impression, and the end of the play left the audience breathless, so stifling was the restraint of accumulated emotion. And when, in 1904, the *Cherry Orchard* was produced, a palpitating hush fell upon the audience after the first curtain, and Chehov's friends had an uneasy feeling that the play was going to be a failure ; but the momentary hesitation was due to a spell of ecstasy that had come over the audience. The next moment the theatre burst into applause. The performance was made an occasion for celebrating the twenty-fifth year of Chehov's literary activity, and he was publicly acclaimed as one of Russia's greatest dramatists. He was cheered by the audience lingeringly and affectionately. In a letter to a friend two days after the event, he says: 'At the first performance of the "Cherry Orchard" on the 17th of January, they gave me an ovation, so lavish, warm, and really so unexpected, that I can't get over it even now...'

His health, in the meanwhile, was declining steadily, and it was clear to many who saw him that his end was not far off. The hearty reception exhausted him, and he returned with relief to his home at Yalta. His health was shattered, and at the beginning of May, 1904, terribly ill, he journeyed to Moscow, and on arrival took to his bed and was laid up till June. In June he set off with his wife for a cure to the Black Forest, and settled in Badenweiler. He wrote to his sister that he was hourly adding weight and steadily getting better and stronger ; it may have been that it was an attempt to deceive himself, or he may have believed it, for he had already begun to make inquiries about the steamers returning to Russia, when, on the 2nd of July, he died.

CHAPTER FOUR

THE MEANS BY WHICH HIS SENSIBILITY WAS GIVEN EXPRESSION: A TECHNICAL EXAMINATION OF HIS STYLE

&I

I COME now to what is, to me, the most attractive section of this essay, to the point at which I may at last, in Mr. Middleton Murry's words, 'conduct a technical examination into the writer's style.' Mr. Arnold Bennett once very properly traced the impulse of the literary art back to what he calls the 'primitive novelist,' who to this day, he says, can be seen transmitting to acquaintances his fragmentary and crude visions of life in the café or the club or the kerbstone: the man who has something to tell and who is bursting to tell it. While the impulse towards communication is also the social justification of literary work, there is poetic justice in the truth that writers who, despite the lack of such an impulse, persist in writing all the same, may conceivably succeed in something very different from good literature: in self-expression to their own, perhaps *entire*, satisfaction. Which does not imply, of course, that a writer either has the impulse for communication or has it not at all: he may have it in varying degree, with varying results. Perhaps that explains why the greater writers have never made half the fuss about the difficulties of delivering themselves of their conceptions as do the smaller ones, who suffer torture in the process of cultivating 'style.' Their admission of their difficulties of expression, which they naïvely think implies a delicate, fastidious, discriminating vision, is not altogether without humour, seeing that what it more clearly implies is a deficiency of that passion for communication that 'sees' the writer 'through' and ensures the delivery of his conceptions in a thoroughly adequate style: in short, a deficiency in genius. Because their sensibilities, however delicate, had not the stronger impulse necessary for *communicating* their impressions about life to other human beings—the genuine literary gift—by which style (the measure of success of this communication), by completely blending with the writer's own impression of what his work ought to be like, becomes perfect style, our reputed stylists 'played the sedulous ape' and relied on their 'infinite capacity for taking pains' to stimulate their self-expression. To them, because they lack that natural flush that comes from a quickening of the blood in the literary act of communication, 'style' is a matter of cosmetics, to be applied from without.

The first thing, then, to be said about Chehov's style, is that he had something to tell, that he was really anxious to tell it, and so told it easily and directly and wholly: in perfectly adequate style. The 'problem' of *how* simply did not arise.

& II

Then there is Realism. Chehov's realism is the natural development of the realism of Gogol, Turgenev, Dostoevski, and Tolstoy; and it differs from the older realism in that he has found for it a new and more consistent form.

Realism, that much-abused term, means, or should mean if it is to mean anything at all, the extracting from life of its characteristic features—for life outside the focus of art is like the sea, blurred, formless, and with no design—and the replacing of them in a design calculated to represent, within art's focus, life that is like the sea, blurred, formless, and with no design. The realist is he who has succeeded in presenting within the orbit of artistic form (without which there can be no question of art) that which eludes form, is formless. In other words, a realist, in the person of Anton Chehov, has, for once, succeeded in actually capturing that wild beast of the jungle—reality—and, moreover, has succeeded in presenting him to us, not caged up in a zoo, but at large in his native wilds: the cage (form) being, for the first time in the history of realistic literature, completely invisible. No one, not the beast himself, is aware of the cage that holds him, because he does not feel the strain, he does not know the difference: and yet he is definitely captured, he cannot get away, he is there before our very eyes, to be gazed upon as long as we may like.

Mr. Arnold Bennett has said somewhere that the odds are against any novel happening in real life. That is not wholly true: the odds are against any crude, rounded-off, symmetrical sort of novel happening in real life. Real life has plots innumerable; but they are subtle. Henry James has a story which illustrates (unconsciously) the misplaced kind of subtlety, subtlety which is positively offensive in the face of the symmetrical crudity of plot that it tries to cloak. A good-looking youth gets engaged to an ugly girl, finds he cannot stand it, and runs away at the last moment. Years later he meets her again. She has now grown beautiful, is the mother of a good-looking son; he, the father of an ugly daughter. The parents bring them together, to make up for their lost opportunity. Her son finds he cannot stand it, runs away at the last moment, as in the first case also, to Paris, where, by a chance, the older man meets him. One may well ask, what is the use of cloaking such a skeleton of symmetry, improbable in real life, with fine shades and subtle trifles, if the latter must needs reveal the initial crudity of the concoction ? Another tale of James's is about a statesman who has no private life, a situation which is, of course, counterbalanced by a novelist who has no public life. This is not subtlety : it is a mental straining. Such plots occur to one by the hundred : you reject them automatically because your instinct tells you that these clockwork motives are not subtlety at all, but merely crudities in miniature. Subtlety in literature runs with and alongside of life ; it has an organic existence ; it is of the same stuff as life ; it has a taste, a smell, you feel better when you come across it. A good deal of James's subtlety runs contrariwise to the 'feel' of life ; it is cold ; it cuts across the tissues of organic life ; it is like the wrong sort of tonic. And those who regard his psychological manufactures as subtle are really marvelling at the fineness of the needle, forgetting that it is but a crowbar in miniature. For 'subtlety' divorced from life is only a matter of manufacture, a matter of size. You turn out nails—big nails, small nails, but they are nails, not tissues. And that is the difference. When we admire him we are in fact admiring artificial flowers. There is no harm in admiring artificial flowers. It is only when we deceive ourselves by thinking that they are real flowers, or, on being disillusioned, boldly declare that they are better than real flowers, that we are on false ground, for then we are divorcing art from the living soil on which it thrives.

Chehov knew that the only plots that are worth anything are those taken directly from life. For they are plots that have grown out of real human psychology, and are for that reason interesting, because they are instructive. 'You can invent anything you like,' Tolstoy once said, 'but you can't invent psychology.' Before Chehov there were realists like Turgenev and Tolstoy, whose context as well as plot were taken from real life, but while their context was always subtle, their plot was always simple. On the other hand, writers like James, whose context was accurate and minute, strove also to make their plots accurate and minute. This they certainly were. But they were not *subtle*. Chehov, pursuing the realism of Tolstoy to its logical conclusion, raised his plots to the standard of his context: blending them into one subtle whole. There is this passage in his story, *The Steppe*:

> Life is terrible and miraculous, and therefore no matter how awful the tale you relate in Russia, no matter how you may adorn it with brigands' nests, long knives, and miracles, it will resound like a myth in the soul of the hearer, and only one who has given way to reading will perhaps glance askance, incredulous, and even he will keep silent. The cross by the road, the dark loaded carts, the open space, and the fate of the men who had gathered around the fire—all this in itself was so miraculous and terrible that the fantastic myths or tales faded and merged with life.

The essential difference, then, between the old tradition and the new one (of which Chehov is the pioneer), is that, whereas of old the fluidness of life as it is really lived and felt was all but overlooked and sometimes forced in order to round off the form and to sharpen the outline of a particular story, in Chehov it is just the fluidness of life that is in fact at once the form and context of his stories, the vitality of form depending on the clarity with which he shows us that the fusion of form and context is deliberate.

When Gorki as a young man submitted to Chehov, then in his forties, a play that he had written, Chehov wrote: 'It is, as I expected, very good, written *à la* Gorki, original, very interesting ; and, to begin by talking of the defects, I have noticed only one, a defect incorrigible as red hair in a red-haired man—the conservatism of the form. You make new and original people sing new songs to an accompaniment that looks second-hand.' Chehov makes the writer Trigorin in the *Sea-Gull* say : '. . . new forms. . . But there's room enough for all, new forms and old forms—why jostle ? ' Of course, the youth who advocated ' new forms ' in the *Sea-Gull* had in mind the symbolic school *à la* Andreiev ; at least the youth's own play inclined towards that kind of thing. (And of Andreiev Chehov says that he is pretentious, difficult to understand, and that his talent reminds one of an artificial nightingale.) When Chehov told Gorki that his play suffered from the conservatism of form, he certainly did not wish Gorki to emulate Andreiev or the youth in the *Sea-Gull.* But he was probably conscious of Gorki's failure to profit by Chehov's own notable contribution to literature—an expedient by means of which literature could succeed in being truly realistic ; in other words, of a form that was actually indistinguishable from the context and yet was clearly manifest.

How did he do it ? Not by dispensing with plot, but by using a totally different kind of plot, the tissues of which, as in life, lie below the surface of events, and, unobtrusive, shape our destiny. Thus he all but overlooks the event-plot ; more, he deliberately lets it be as casual as it is in real life. Before Chehov realism was no more than a convention. Realistic literature had begun to bear a closer resemblance to real life as it piled on more and more certain superficial irrelevancies characteristic of real life. But even in Flaubert, even in Turgenev, even in Tolstoy himself, it stuck to the old traditional form of a strong skeleton plot. The ' story ' which they endeavoured to soak in reality was the better for it; but it was the 'story,' the symmetry, the conclusiveness, the so evidently calculated design of it, that prevented the complete illusion of real life. It was this that made Mr. Bennett say that realism could be no more than a convention. (The other argument that realism is merely a convention because no two persons see 'reality' alike is not serious; for on the same ground everything, even a photograph, is a distortion of reality, since it has to be looked at through a pair of individual eyes.) And it was precisely this that Chehov meant when he complained of Gorki's 'conservatism of form.' It was as if the older realists were afraid to dispense with their 'story' lest their novel should thereby completely lose all sense of form. And so it would, because to them the form depended almost solely on the event-plot. The object of realistic literature was obviously to resurrect the complete illusion of real life by means of things characteristic of real life. But while the older realists were making the details of their stories characteristic of real life, they forgot to make the plot characteristic of real life; so much so that Mr. Bennett once confessed that, so far as the story was concerned, the odds were against any novel happening in real life. Chehov saw that, and made his plots characteristic of real life by choosing for his themes stories which were not of the unlikely kind (because taken from real life and developed into 'stories'), but just as they would probably have happened if allowed to run their natural course in real life. Thus the odds are not against but for Chehov's stories happening in real life. Because, whereas the other realists had to convince us that their story happened in real life against such a probability, Chehov's story is to convince us that the same story did in fact *not* happen as the other novelists would have us think it did, but was at this or that point blurred, interrupted, mauled, or otherwise tampered with (as most 'would-be' stories are in real life) by life: the making it all as much as possible real life and as little as possible a 'story' is, in fact, the story —the plot completely blended with the context, and the form accentuated by the feeling, 'This is life.' To Chehov literature is life made intelligible by the discovery of form—the form that is invisible in life but which is seen when, mentally, you step aside to get a better view of life. Life, because it has aspects innumerable, seems blurred and devoid of all form. And since literature must have form, and life has none, realists of the past thought that they could not paint life in the aggregate and preserve form, and thus saw fit to express one aspect of life at a time. Until a wholly new aspect occurred to Chehov—that of life in the aggregate: which aspect, in truth, is his form.

Chehov has written no novels. He called *The Duel* a novel, but it is really too short for a novel. But that he wrote short and long stories should not be taken to mean that his method of dispensing with the visible event-plot was unsuitable for the novel. The formula for the modern novel and story, short or long, would be something like this: That things—psychological, 'atmospheric,' and other—must arise out of one another with, and to, some significance. The longer the story, therefore, the more space there is for things, for more things, to arise out of one another—even to a greater significance. This formula would mean that the novel has both form and plot—though both may be implicit rather than obtrusive. But the value of such formulæ is more apparent than real. They are statements of things a writer has to clear up in his own mind sometime or another. Masterpieces will be written despite, not because of, such considerations. Art, literature, are gentle things. They should not be squeezed too hard to suit existing definitions. The writer is himself one quarter unaware as to whither he is steering. It is the critics who will afterwards discover ' tendencies ' and rules and method and hidden implications. A work of art whose aim and meaning were quite clear to the writer in the act of writing it would perish, as the universe would perish if its aim were clearly known to it. How, indeed, can we determine lasting formulæ for art if art can have no life outside the unexpected ?

& III

But to take a few practical examples. ' To put up with the established fact was impossible, not to put up with it was also impossible, and there was no middle course.' So thought the young man whose sister had run off with a neighbour [*Neighbours.*] The mother was in hysterics. The aunt was making the question of her departure depend on the incident. At length, having made up his mind, the young man rode over to the neighbour, fully intent on settling the question one way or the other. He was going to insult the man, whatever the consequences. But when he arrived at the neighbour's house he was disarmed by the ready confidences and the meek manner of his former friend. The more he saw and heard, the more he understood, and the more he understood, the more he was baffled, till he had almost forgotten what he had come for. Instead of acting as he had intended, the brother finds himself listening to long, drawn-out reminiscences of his sister's seducer, which are humorous enough because the man gives himself away so completely. He tells about his early marriage—a strange affair, in the manner of Dostoevski. It is, in fact, a sort of momentary parody of Dostoevski. Chehov's touch here is delightfully malicious. It appears that he had married a poor unfortunate girl who had been wronged and abandoned by a brother officer, and he was therefore asked to leave the regiment, which he did with pride in his heart. He was an inefficient idealist, utterly devoid of any sense of humour. He experienced, in his own words, some pure, exalted moments. The poor girl, however, whom he had married from the highest motives, lost all respect for him the moment she became his wife. 'A clever man has chucked me,' she used to taunt him, 'and a fool has picked me up!' She went utterly to the bad after marriage, left him, but remained a source of great trouble and expense, for he was still sending money to her while she was having a good time with local officers. He was very tall, thin, consumptive, and ungainly, and lacked every conceivable gift except sincerity, and it is because he gives himself away in his narration, without in the least suspecting it, that his dull autobiography is so thrilling. He was heavily in debt, his estate had been mortgaged twice over, and as he was short of fuel, he used the wooden railing round the house for firewood. But withal he had a lofty mind and was addicted to liberal principles; but even there he was inefficient and stale, and when he spoke his voice was as monotonous as though he were drawling one solitary note. In the course of the evening he relates a rather gruesome story about a certain Frenchman named Olivier, who many years before had rented the country house, and who had ordered his daughter's supposed lover to be flogged to death and the body thrown into the pond. Thus the evening comes to a close. The sister seems grateful to her brother for having called, for she interprets this as approval on his part. But she is sad, for she knows that her proud mother is heart-broken and will never forgive her; at the same time, for fear of putting herself in the wrong, she will neither return nor ask her mother's forgiveness. The brother is so admirably able to enter into the respective positions of all the persons concerned in the dilemma that he can come to no conclusion at all. His sister and her lover walk with him part of the way home. The ineffectual unhappy seducer talks of the pure, exalted moments they had experienced after dinner when they were reading some dull article together. 'I could not contain myself,' he adds, 'and wrote a letter to the editor for communication to the author. I wrote just one line: "Thank you. I press firmly your honest hand!"' Slowly the brother rides home. 'Olivier,' he thinks, as he passes the pond, 'acted inhumanly, but one way or another he settled the question, while I have settled nothing, but have only made a muddle of it.'

But that he is unable to settle anything, even though aware himself of the practical absurdity of his impotence, is a tribute to his mind, not a blemish. What is an *impasse* to-day may be a practical proposition to-morrow. It is the way of transcendence which, like the imagination, seems to be an 'upward' and unfolding impetus. Even if our perception of fine shades in human conduct may at times frustrate solution, it is no indictment of a discriminating vision. The implication is that creative evolution works on the lines of the imagination—half blindly. Something without yields; our will sees an opening and pushes in a wedge. Thus we transcend. Therefore we cannot blindly trust the law of contradiction, even though it may pretend to 'settle things' more easily.

In *The Story of an Unknown Person* Chehov approaches life from two opposite angles: he presents to us, in the persons of two intelligent young men, the contrast between the active and the passive modes of vision. He adds a young woman fired by vague idealism, who first throws over her husband from the highest motives of free-love and vague idealism, but after being jilted by the lover with whom, much to his annoyance, she goes to live, she leaves him also, discovering that he too has no ideals, and becomes attached to the fiery ex-naval officer who, for revolutionary reasons, has been masquerading as a valet in the employ of her lover—on the ground that he at least has an active vision and clear ideals. Together, they set out abroad, where she is to discover that her new friend, under the influence of failing health and sunny Italy, has tired of his active revolutionary ideals and only craves for a passive life of comfort and tranquillity.

The treatment of the theme is made the more ironic because Chehov tells the story through the mouth of the man of action. Thus the man of passive vision comes in for a good deal of censure, and particularly in the impassioned letter which the pseudo-valet writes to his employer on the eve of his own departure, in which he discloses his true identity and denounces in fiery words his employer's 'asiatic' sloth and love of comfort, his cold ironic attitude to life and people, and his idle lack of aim. It was a passionate, beautiful letter enough. But then Chehov's irony is a warm, understanding, kindly irony, for he can sympathize with either view, as well as with the young woman. This is just what is so peculiarly attractive about Chehov's touch: that he can clothe a plot of naked irony with pity and human understanding. At the end of the story the disquieting impartiality, the *impasse* of Chehov's sensibility, is lucidly expressed in the conversation that takes place between the two men. After the death of the young woman in child-birth—there had been the suspicion that she had poisoned herself—the ex-revolutionary returns to Petersburg in order that he might arrange with his late employer for the future of the latter's child. During an interview, in the course of which the question of the little daughter is satisfactorily settled, the host recalls his pseudo-valet's fiery screed, and they exchange these views upon the subject:

'You have probably already forgotten your letter. But I cherish it. Your mood then I understand and, let me confess, I respect that letter. Cold, cursed blood, asiatic, horse laughter—this is nice and characteristic,' he continued, smiling ironically. 'And the main idea is probably near the truth, though one could argue without end. That is to say,' he shuffled, 'argue not with the idea itself, but with your attitude to the question, with your temperament, so to speak. Yes, my life is abnormal, spoilt, and no good, and what prevents me from beginning a new life is cowardice—here you are perfectly right. But that you should be taking this so much to heart, that you should be excited and in despair—that's no reason, there you are quite wrong.'

'A living man can't help getting excited and being in despair when he sees how he is perishing and how others around him are perishing.'

'Who says so! I'm not preaching indifference in the least, but only want an objective attitude to life. The more objective, the less danger there is of making mistakes. One must look into the root and seek in each event the cause of all causes. We have grown weak, we have come down, finally we have fallen, our generation consists entirely of neurotics, grousers, all we do is talk of being tired, worn-out, but neither you nor I are responsible for it; we are too small a fry for the fate of a whole generation to depend on our arbitrary acts. Here, it must be supposed, there are big, general causes, which, from the biological point of view, have their solid *raison d'être*. We are neurotics, sour people, funks, but perhaps this is necessary and useful for those generations who are going to live after us. Not a hair falls from the head without the will of the Heavenly Father—in other words, in nature and the sphere of mankind nothing happens for no reason. All is reasonable and necessary. And if so, why should we get unduly excited and write desperate letters ?'

'That is so,' I said thoughtfully. 'I believe that the following generations will have it easier and will see better, having profited by our experience. But one also wants to live independently of the future generations, and not merely for their sake. Life is given but once, and one wants to live it gladly, significantly, beautifully. One wants to play a conspicuous, noble part, one wants to make history, in order that the same generations should have no right to say of every one of us : That was a nonentity, or even worse. . . I believe in the purpose and necessity of what happens around us, but what concern have I with that necessity, why should my " I " perish ?'

'Well, what's to be done !' sighed Orlov, rising and, as it were, showing that our conversation was already at an end.

I picked up my cap.

To take another plot—*A Woman's Kingdom*. A young heiress, of peasant blood but of refined education, comes across an attractive and hard-working foreman who happens to be employed in one of her own factories, and gradually conceives the idea of marrying him. After dinner on Christmas Day, in a particularly happy mood, she descends to the kitchen, where all the hangers-on—a host of women, young and old—are gathered, and, encouraged by the lively talk of some stray old woman, actually confesses before them all her wish to marry the foreman, and almost enlists the services of one of the women to bring about the marriage. Going up to the drawing-room, in a mood of happy melancholy, she sits down to the piano, plays and sings, and her silly young butler brings up the tea, with a stupid grin on his face. She asks him why he is grinning. He says that he is amused at the joke of her wanting to marry the foreman. She looks at him, incredulous : Why ? Because, says the man, it tickles him to think of the foreman sitting side by side with his Excellency and the other gentleman, who had been dining that night. 'Why,' he grins again, 'he doesn't even know how to hold a fork properly.' And in an instant her illusion is shattered to fragments. She feels the pity of it, she is disappointed with herself and him, cries for her lost happiness of a moment since, but now cannot consider the marriage, and warns the matchmaker that her declared intention of a while ago was only a joke.

This is a bare plot, but it is so completely lost in, indeed identified with, the very taste and smell of life that exudes from the context of the story that its form, while free from any trace of artificial *outline*, is obtained from within by that blending unifying sense: that here we have a picture of real life with its outwardly irrational drama which privately we all admit to be most potent. The life that is portrayed within the compass of his story is at once loyal to the purpose of the story and loyal to the truth of life without.

Her chamber-maid is hopelessly in love with the butler, and because both women have been done out of their seeming happiness, they understand each other without words. 'Silly fools we are, both of us,' says the young heiress, crying and laughing. 'Silly fools! Oh, what silly fools!'

The Teacher of Literature affords a good example for a technical examination of a Chehov plot. It is the story of a young pedagogue's elopement. Up to the last page or so everything is pure unmitigated bliss for the young man, till in the end he tires and revolts from the sheer abundance of it. This is, briefly, how Chehov puts it together. When Nikitin (the young teacher) used to visit the home of the girl he was afterwards to marry, we are shown some seemingly trivial but actually outstanding features that impress themselves upon our mind. There was her father, rather in the background, always talking to somebody, and always one could hear him saying: 'It's loutishness! Loutishness, and nothing else. Yes, loutishness!' There were dogs, one of which seemed to dislike Nikitin, and growled at him, in this manner: 'rrr . . . nga-nga-nga-nga . . . rrr . . .' while the other had the nasty habit of laying his wet muzzle on Nikitin's trousers. Then there was the elder sister, a clever but domineering girl of twenty-three, who took the place of her dead mother. 'She called herself an old maid—which meant that she was confident that she would marry.' And there was a certain Captain Polyanski who paid court to her. Nikitin shares a flat with an elderly colleague, whose chief characteristic throughout is that he is always saying things which are very obvious.

When Nikitin, roused by the rather high-handed ways of the elder daughter, shouts back at her: 'I'm not going to argue any more. There'll be no end to it! Enough!' he immediately exclaims: 'Oh, go away, you confounded dog!' for the big dog has laid his wet muzzle and paw on Nikitin's knees, while 'rrr . . . nga-nga-nga-nga . . .' issues from under the chair hiding the small dog. 'It's loutishness!' he hears their father's voice from the other end of the table. 'I said so to the Governor himself. This, your Excellency, I said, is loutishness!'

Nikitin gets engaged to the younger daughter, who, though not as handsome as her elder sister, is extremely pleasant and attractive, while Captain Polyanski still pays his attentions to the elder girl. Then there was the wedding and Nikitin was married, and in his diary he notes down that in the last few years everything, even the weather, has been serving the single purpose of his happiness. As he was being congratulated in church, his colleague, the teacher who always said what was very obvious, came up to him and said: 'So far you were unmarried and lived alone, and now you are married and will live together.' From church they drove to the new house, which had come to Nikitin, among other things, as part of his wife's dowry. Guests and relatives were drinking champagne and the band was playing flourishes, and the elder sister suddenly began to laugh and cry, and then fainted. 'Nobody can understand!' she muttered. 'Nobody, nobody! Oh, my God! nobody can understand!'

But everybody understood quite well, that she was older than her sister Manya by four years, but was still not married, and that she cried, not because she was jealous, but from a melancholy recognition that her time was passing, and perhaps had already passed. When they were dancing the cadril, she was already back in the ballroom, with a tear-stained and heavily powdered face, and I [it is from Nikitin's diary] saw how Captain Polyanski was holding before her a plate of ice-cream, while she ate with a little spoon.

Married life was to Nikitin the consummation of the earlier happiness of the days of his engagement. His young wife proved to be a most efficient house-wife into the bargain. Their life was an idyll.

He incessantly watched how his clever, clear-headed Manya built the nest, and wanting to show her that he too was not superfluous in the house, he would go and do something useless: for instance, pull the dog-cart out of the shed and examine it all over. Manya started a real dairy with three cows, and in the cellars she had lots of jugs of milk and pots of sour cream, and all this she kept for butter.

Life to him was an idyll. But he told his wife that he was the maker of his own happiness, and he expressed the view that the miseries and deprivations of his childhood and the loneliness of his youth had earned him the right to enjoy this happiness. He even forgot that he owed his material prosperity largely to his wife. But that he loved her (Chehov will never press a point too far) is evidenced by this:

> That which in her words was just, seemed to him uncommon, extraordinary; and that which differed from his own convictions was, in his view, naïve and touching.

The narrative goes on in this deliberately casual way:

> In October the school sustained a heavy loss: Ippolit Ippolitich [the old colleague] was taken ill with erysipelas on the head and died. For two days before his death he was unconscious and delirious, but even in his delirium he said nothing that was not perfectly well known to everyone.
>
> 'The Volga flows into the Caspian Sea. . . Horses eat oats and hay.'

The old teacher died of erysipelas, but the funeral was very solemn and lavish; and there is this mild ironic touch:

> And looking at the solemn funeral, passers-by crossed themselves and said:
>
> 'God grant everyone to die like that.'

Another subtle touch is the way in which Chehov shows us Nikitin's selfish narrowness (which is at the core of the whole story) by making him, on his return from the funeral, set down in his diary this unconsciously self-depreciative passage: 'I wanted to say a warm word at my colleague's grave, but I was warned that this might displease the Headmaster, as he did not like our poor friend.'

The winter was drab and wet, but, despite the bad weather, Nikitin was as happy as in the summer. Only one thing annoyed him: the cats and dogs that he had received as part of the dowry. The cats fought the dogs, and there was a smell in the room like in a zoo, and the small dog still hated him and would not acknowledge him as his master, and growled at him: ' rrr . . . nga-nga-nga...'

One night as he returned from his club, where he had lost twelve roubles playing cards, his thoughts were gloomy, and he began to reproach himself for his undeserved happiness; indeed, he began to feel that personal happiness was not only illegitimate in itself, but simply could not last. He became dissatisfied with his work, for which he now saw he had no qualifications; he began to crave for some new work in which he could lose himself entirely, to the extent of indifference to his personal happiness, the sensation of which, he began to feel, was so boringly monotonous. When he came home his wife was already asleep, and the white cat lay on her quilt. When he spoke to her, from underneath the bed the small dog growled: ' rrr . . . nga-nga-nga...' She told him that her elder sister had been to see her that night. He knew that Captain Polyanski, on whom latterly her sister had strongly counted, had been transferred to another province, ' She hasn't said anything,' his wife told him, ' but one can see by her face how hard it is for her, poor thing.'

Next day at dinner there was his father-in-law and the elder sister. She had tear-stained eyes and complained of a headache, while their father ate a lot and spoke of how the young men nowadays were unreliable and how little gentlemanly feeling there was in them.

' It's loutishness! ' he said. ' I shall tell him so to his face. " It's loutishness, sir," I shall say.'

Nikitin smiled and played the host. But after dinner he went to his study and locked himself in.

Spring was beginning as exquisitely as last spring, and it promised the same joys... But Nikitin was thinking that it would be nice to take a holiday and go to Moscow, and stay at his old lodgings there. In the next room they were drinking coffee and talking of Captain Polyanski, while he tried not to listen, and wrote in his diary: 'Where am I, my God? I am surrounded by vulgarity and vulgarity. Wearisome, insignificant people, pots of sour cream, jugs of milk, cockroaches, stupid women. . . There is nothing more terrible, mortifying, and distressing than vulgarity. I must flee from here, flee to-day, or I shall go out of my mind!'

In this synopsis I have tried to indicate the chief threads on which the story hangs. I have mentioned only a few of the recurring *motifs* which, taken all together, go to the making of that process of completely blending context with plot which is, perhaps, the most distinctive feature of Chehov's method of construction. But it is sufficient to assume that the story has, besides the few main threads I have indicated, innumerable minor threads, to understand precisely why by blending plot and context Chehov manages to give a rejuvenating living touch to the vision of reality, which lifts his work out of the ruck of those realistic writers whose realism is necessarily only a convention.

&IV

Mr. F. M. Hueffer, writing in the *English Review*, is beside himself with joy because he thinks *Ulysses* is certain to determine the fate of modern Anglo-Saxon literature upon the psychological road. There is the inevitable allusion to Dostoevski. All of which is very nice. But when one hears it suggested that Mr. Joyce is fast catching up with Dostoevski, it might be not irrelevant to remark that since the time of Dostoevski psychological literature so-called has taken considerable strides in the method of one Anton Chehov. And for these reasons. Firstly (as already shown), he has found for it a suitable artistic form. Secondly, while making us feel unceasingly aware of the magnitude of psychological experience, he does not indulge in twenty-four-hour days of it, but through stressing some reactions he gives psychology a sense of form. And, thirdly, the psychological experiences he gives us are all either significantly perturbing or delightful, or both, and delightful even when intrinsically dull because of the ingenious way in which he manages to bring them in. Dostoevski's novels, on the other hand, were all rather clumsy on account of the hasty carelessness with which he narrated his event-plot—a survival of the old conservative method of narration—which at times seemed almost distinct from, and merely introductory to, the cherished psychological effects which he was about to make, and one often feels as if he were himself impatient of the necessity of such a preliminary narration. Nor is his presentation of psychology in itself delightful, and he seems unable to combine, as Chehov can, seriousness of purpose with delight. Psychology, in any case, is not yet literature. It is sometimes an easy means of getting away. The lack of the true artistic gift is not so apparent in a tangle of complex psychological threads as it was in the straightforward narrative. Psychological literature, instead of recording clear and single motives, as in the ' stories ' of the past, has to give expression to a ' system ' of complex reactions, something after this manner: I talk to A., and, while conscious of him, something might suggest to me B., and then something else might send the thought coursing through my mind that I haven't paid my dentist's bill, while all the time I may be conscious of the pointed shape of A.'s shoes, which suddenly brings home to me the exact atmosphere of a certain summer morning in Calcutta, while I calmly assent to A.'s proposition. This is, in effect, how we do live, and

Russian literature ever since Gogol has been acknowledging it more and more as the complex ' feel ' of life. But perhaps, either in order to make up for the long and persistent abstinence on the part of English realism, or for some unknown reason, Mr. Joyce has now outdone all the Russians put together, so much so that distinguished critics wave their hands in a panic and declare that Mr. Joyce is either a stupendous genius or he is nothing. But in either case it will take them ten or fifteen years to think about it, and indeed they doubt whether the question can be settled satisfactorily at all in a few generations. It is, as a matter of fact, not always true that posterity is the best judge of literary values. Posterity may be completely out of tune with the mood that necessitated the expression of a work of literature, and be unjust to it. What are scholars for, if not to reconstruct for themselves a past atmosphere in which alone it *was* possible to appreciate the expression of a certain phase and aspect of life of which the work is an outcome, and thus get the better of the disadvantage (which we commonly think an advantage !) of belonging to ' posterity ' in relation to a dead man's work of literature ? Thus certain trends in writing can be profitably discussed in our own lifetime. There is no limit to the recording of complex experiences of a twelve, twenty-four, or thirty-six-hour day, or, for that matter, of a continuous, indefinite experience. The real objection is that such recording, however faithful, is not interesting in itself. It is not interesting—it is boring—for me to follow the minute complex reflections of my continuous consciousness, but it is tolerable because, after all, seeing that I exist, I am more or less concerned with my own sensations. But it is positively tedious for me to follow the minute record (in staccato sentences) of the ordinary sensations of another person unless I have reason to be interested in that person: and it is up to the author to make me so—an end which he is more likely to achieve by a partially objective attitude to that person. (The same applies to the handling of 'indecencies' in literature. No one is shocked by his own indecencies; but what is indecent is to read of other people's. A man might eat like a pig and be happy, but the sight of another person eating like himself might spoil his appetite.) There is probably nothing easier than to record minutely one's continuous reactions to casual experiences during the day. But even granted that an experiment of this kind needs a perceptive mind, it is not plain how it is necessarily a matter of art and literature. Such painstaking record of psychological reactions resembles the frequent taking of a patient's temperature. If it is literature, then the psychologist ought to be the crowning novelist, in the absence of all other gifts. But he is not. Because to the novelist psychology is a means, not an end in itself, rough material to be fashioned into art, not yet art. It is no more than a commodity, like paint to a painter. Literature, whether the material be psychological or otherwise, needs taste and tact and humour. It needs discrimination, proportion, and restraint. Above all humour, without which the vision of life is devoid of the component that ensures a sane sense of proportion. This is the reason why it is pretty useless at this time of day to talk of Dostoevski, Mr. Joyce, and the psychological novel, while completely ignoring the artistic advance in the handling of psychology made by Anton Chehov. Chehov does not give us a cross-section of a lump of life, taken, as it were, at random, by merely registering the irrelevant perceptions which make it up. Chehov—because he is an artist as well as a psychologist—discriminates in his choice of those seeming irrelevancies which in literature go to the making of the illusion of real life, for he feels that by economizing in dullness he heightens our delight; and he does it all by killing as many birds as possible with one stone.

Thus when he introduces an irrelevancy, it is always one of those seeming irrelevancies which are, in point of actual result, significant relevancies. For he charges each with several tasks. (*a*) To connote by its apparent irrelevancy the illusion of real life: it is so in real life, we think of one thing and then our thought goes off at a tangent. (*b*) To be in itself amusing, delightful, pathetic, tragic, or otherwise beautiful. (*c*) To be always significant, that is psychologically true, throwing additional light on the character as well as on his subjective existence. (*d*) To consolidate the form of the story by bringing in, if possible, the same apparent irrelevancy more than once—by making it characteristic of a person. And, above all (*e*), by emphasizing some irrelevancies at the expense of others to bring the reader to a point at which he can see where these more prominent irrelevancies (already transformed by the concerted functions of *a*, *b*, *c*, and *d* into throbbing psychological threads) touch upon the fading threads of others in the background. Thus psychology is used by him for artistic ends. He shapes it into something at once beautiful and significant and perturbing, and yet true to life, something we call art. Even if he is little conscious of the process, and his final vision coincides with his initial vision, he has been seeing art, the possibility of art in human psychology, not psychology alone. The difference is worth noting.

But to take a concrete example—from *The Teacher of Literature*. During a dance an elderly 'cultured' gentleman comes up to Nikitin, the young teacher, and in the course of flattering conversation asks him if he has read Lessing's dramatic criticism.

'No, I haven't.'

Shebaldin was horrified and waved his hands as though he had burnt his fingers, and ,without uttering a word, backed away from Nikitin. Shebaldin's form, his question and amazement struck Nikitin as funny, but he thought nevertheless :

'It is rather awkward. I, a teacher of literature, have not read Lessing. I must read him.'

That night, on returning to his flat, Nikitin lay on the sofa in his study and thought of the time when he would be married, and suddenly fell asleep. He dreamt, among other things, how he walked in the town garden with his future wife.

Here he saw oak-trees and crows' nests, which looked like caps. One nest swung. Shebaldin looked out of it and shouted loudly : 'You haven't read Lessing ! '

Nikitin's whole body started, and he opened his eyes.

After he had proposed marriage to his future wife, Nikitin returns home, at the height of happiness.

He undressed quickly and quickly got into bed, in order to begin as soon as possible to think of his happiness, of Manusya, of the future ; he smiled and suddenly remembered that he hadn't yet read Lessing.

'I must read him . . .' he thought. 'Though, what should I read him for ? Be hanged with him ! '

And, tired out by his happiness, he went to sleep immediately and smiled till morn.

Towards the end of the story, in a mood of profound dissatisfaction with himself, feeling that he had become stale and smug in his puny little world of personal happiness, he began to long for work which would raise his self-respect:

And in his imagination suddenly, as though alive, the clean-shaven Shebaldin grew up and spoke in horror :

'You haven't read even Lessing! How backward you are! God, how low you have fallen!'

This is but an irrelevancy—one out of a multitude—but how relevant! and not least so because its function also is to demonstrate the seemingly irrelevant nature of our manner of thinking.

If literature is to be as large as life, we must focus that largeness of it within a small recognizable orbit. To have a real idea of the limitless, formless sea as it is, we must see it in perspective, like the painter who had thus depicted it within the four corners of a frame. Whereas the psychological procedure of seeing life—in the absence of the guiding instinct for perspective and proportion: the determining artistic gift, whatever the medium—would be to set down the chemical properties of a cross-section of the ocean.

One sometimes reads of a popular novelist who, having succumbed to the trend of the age, but without knowing much about the matter, tries his hand at the 'psychological novel.' And then one reads, years later, that Mr. X. has returned to the simple, straightforward task of telling a *story* (with a human interest!), upon which course the popular literary paper congratulates him. Well, a story has no human interest unless it be psychological. But it is probably the best thing that he can do if he cannot see that literature is a matter of perspective: that, provided you do not enumerate your psychological subtleties, but conceive them in the perspective of your story, a psychological story will be the richest and most interesting of all. To dabble loosely in psychology and to set it down in a casual and disconnected manner is no great matter. Other writers than Chehov have done that. But to perceive life, with all its subtleties, in a cumulative unity, where all the diverse-coloured rays meet and yet merge imperceptibly at both ends into the rest of life, needs a lens like his.

&V

Much of the appeal of Chehov, it must be confessed, is irrevocably lost in translation. Some gestures of speech, some poses and idiosyncrasies, are so absolutely inseparable from the Russian language and custom and atmosphere that you cannot render them in any other tongue. But that Chehov's method need not be confined to his country cannot be doubted. Any writer—given the requisite talent—could practise it in any country, any language, with results that would open the reading public's eyes. But, so far, it seems that only Katherine Mansfield was alive to the intrinsic value of Chehov's method. For she alone, with a flavour all her own, invites comparison with Chehov's method of using psychology for artistic ends. They have shown us that subtlety can be expressed easily and directly. They have none of James's strings of definitions, qualifications, amplifications, ramifications, curtailments, which remind one of a tailor who, fumbling with his scissors, first cuts off a slice but not enough, then cuts off too much and is obliged to add a piece—and yet, perhaps in consideration of the pains he takes, is acclaimed a subtle craftsman. It is at the garment we must look. Chehov has managed to express subtle things simply. Henry James has succeeded in expressing simple things subtly. But it is the broth that matters, not the act of stewing it, which with James seems to take place in public. In Chehov we see nothing of the seething process, which is in the secret furnace of his sensibility. And, once the broth is stewed, he serves it out to us simply and directly. 'You have so many qualifications,' he writes to

Gorki, ' that you strain the reader's attention and tire him. It is easy to understand when I write " A man sat down on the grass " ; easy because it is clear and does not keep back one's attention. On the other hand, it is not easy to understand, and a bit hard for the brain, if I write : " A tall, slim, medium-sized man with a ruddy beard sat down on the green, already trampled grass, sat down noiselessly, staring round him timidly and nervously. . ." This does not settle down in the brain at once, and fiction should settle down at once, in a second.'

In common with Tolstoy, he had that intuitive knack of hitting on the apt and usually irrelevant and yet peculiarly significant detail by which somehow we recognize real life in literature. Gogol, for example, had a very different method ; he indulged freely in detailed description. Tolstoy's and Chehov's method was that of flinging in the apt descriptive detail in a swift and unobtrusive manner. Gogol might describe in detail the wall-paper of a room. In *Anna Karenina* the wall-paper is not mentioned for its own sake. But when Anna is desperately ill she stares at the wall-paper and notices its details with a peculiar, irrational interest. This is, we somehow feel, true to life ; it is significant of life. It is an apparent triviality such as signifies great literature. And it is because Tolstoy's and Chehov's works are permeated with this kind of thing that we feel the pulse of life in them. This quality Chehov has in common with Tolstoy, but specializing in it more than the older writer, Chehov's objects are even more delicately charged with emotional significance. When Gurov, in *The Lady with the Dog*, reached the town in which his mistress lived, he 'took the best room at the hotel, in which the floor was covered with grey army cloth, and on the table was an inkstand, grey with dust and adorned with a figure on horseback, with its hat in its hand and its head broken off.' Now Gurov was love-sick and anxious, for the circumstances of his impending meeting with his mistress were uncertain and precarious. She was a young married woman living with her husband, and she did not know of Gurov's arrival in her town. They had parted over a year ago, and now he had arrived in the hope of meeting her again. The significance of the apparently irrelevant 'inkstand, grey with dust and adorned with a figure on horseback, with its hat in its hand and its head broken off' is the same as that of the wall-paper in Tolstoy's *Anna Karenina.* In moments of excitement, when the heart beats faster, we are prone to notice irrelevant things. In those moments it so often happens that the things we come across are humorous or grotesque. And as we read this detail of the inkstand thrown across the love-path, not only do we visualize the scene more keenly, but also feel that the disquiet which he feels is focused for the moment on this chance but very particular inkstand, that it claims attention in his animation, goes to the making of the peculiar atmosphere by which afterwards he will recall it (unless the thought of it will reconstruct for him the atmosphere), as his heart beats faster at the thought of the impending meeting. And, deceived by the life-like quality of a piece of prose, our hearts too beat faster, as though we ourselves were living through it.

& VI

'The descriptions of nature are fine,' he writes of Turgenev in a letter, 'but . . . I feel that we have already got out of the way of such descriptions and that we need something different.' Chehov must have been aware that the various branches of art, though more or less interdependent, are at their best when they encroach least upon one another's prerogatives. His works bear testimony to it. He recognized that it was always a bad practice, for example, to compete with painting in a minute description of a landscape, dress, room, or face, and so forth. There were few emotions that one art could convey which another could not render, but a radically different method was needed to secure the same end. It is evident that while in a picture you get the simultaneous effect of detail, detail in a work of literature would have to be enumerated—a painful process, since to describe a landscape by enumerating the shape, colour and position of the things that go to make it up is to ape in writing the method of painting, to the detriment of writing. This would seem obvious enough, since to paint in words that which can be painted with advantage by the brush is like using paint that evaporated on the canvas in the doing. Such 'word-painting' makes an altogether unjustifiable demand on the memory of the reader, who is expected to retain a complete picture of the whole, while the objects that are to make up the atmosphere are given him piecemeal. And yet, even to this day, one reads novels where the author, counting on a prodigious memory in the reader, treats him to a detailed description of a dining-room, by first enumerating the several objects which comprise it, and then the details of each object, at the end of which he tells you their exact positions, after the manner of Mr. Shaw in his stage-directions. Which is boring. But there is no doubt that objects do go towards making up an atmosphere, and there is a way—a *literary* way—of conveying the effect of painting. And, like the effect of painting, it is complete and simultaneous. Again and again Chehov shows us how it can be done. His works provide innumerable examples ; and this is what he has to say upon the subject in the *Sea-Gull*, where he gets the young writer to decry his own old-fashioned method and to praise the (Chehov) method of his rival. 'This description of a moonlight night,' says he, 'is long and stilted. Trigorin has worked out a method of his own, and descriptions are easy for him. He writes of a neck of a broken bottle glittering on the bank, and of a shadow growing black under the mill-wheel—and there you have your moonlight night all complete, while I speak of the shimmering light, the twinkling stars, the distant sounds of a piano melting into the still and scented air.—Which is painful.'

In a letter to another writer Chehov gives the same advice: 'Cut out all those pages about the moonlight, and give us instead what you feel about it—the reflection of the moon in a piece of broken bottle. . .' In a letter to Gorki, on the subject of the latter's stories, Chehov writes: 'Frequent personification (anthropomorphism) when the sea breathes, the sky gazes, the steppe barks, nature whispers, speaks, mourns, and so on—such metaphors make your description somewhat monotonous, sometimes sweetish, sometimes not clear; beauty and expressiveness in nature are attained only by simplicity, by such simple phrases as "The sun set," "It was dark," "It began to rain," and so on.'

Here is a passage from his story *Gusev*, which illustrates Chehov's *literary* method of competing with painting in the expression of nature. In this instance it is the sea that he writes of; and on perusal it will be clear that the whole effect conveyed is one which covers everything that painting could express, and possibly more: that is to say, in addition to the expression of the significance of the sea we also have a swift, simultaneous vision of it before our eyes; but—and that is the difference—he does not, in the interests of literature, encroach upon the sister art: he does not paint in words.

> The two of them, he and the soldier, threaded their way to the head of the ship, then stood at the rail and looked up and down. Overhead deep sky, bright stars, peace and stillness, exactly as at home in the village, below darkness and disorder. The tall waves were resounding, no one could tell why. Whichever wave you looked at, each one was trying to rise higher than all the rest, and to chase and crush the next one; after it a third as fierce and hideous flew noisily, with a glint of light on its white mane.
>
> The sea has no sense and no pity. If the steamer had been smaller and not made of thick iron, the waves would have crushed it to pieces without the slightest compunction, and would have devoured all the people in it with no distinction of saints or sinners. The steamer had the same cruel and meaningless expression. This monster with its huge beak was dashing onward, cutting millions of waves in its path; it had no fear of the darkness nor the wind, nor of space, nor of solitude, caring for nothing, and if the ocean had its people this monster would have crushed them, too, without distinction of saints or sinners.

This is how he writes of a train which has just that moment left a station on a summer evening:

> The station no longer screened off the sunset, the plain lay open before us, but the sun had already set and the smoke lay in black clouds over the green, velvety young corn. It was melancholy in the spring air, and in the darkening sky, and in the railway carriage. [*The Beauties.*]

Or of a train coming in at midday in the summer:

> At last the train came in sight. Coils of perfectly pink smoke from the funnels floated over the copse, and two windows in the last compartment flashed so brilliantly in the sun that it hurt their eyes to look at it. [*Three Years.*]

&VII

Emotional restraint determines Chehov's style. 'The only defect,' he writes to Gorki about the latter's work, 'is the lack of restraint, the lack of grace. When a man spends the least possible number of movements over some definite action, that is grace. One is conscious of superfluity in your expenditure.' Again he writes to Gorki: 'You are like a spectator at the theatre who expresses his transports with so little restraint that he prevents himself and other people from listening. This lack of restraint is particularly felt in the descriptions of nature with which you interrupt your dialogues; when one reads those descriptions one wishes they were more compact, shorter, put into two or three lines. The frequent mention of tenderness, whispering, velvetiness, and so on, gives those descriptions a rhetorical and monotonous character—and they make one feel cold and almost exhaust one. The lack of restraint is felt also in the descriptions of women and love-scenes. It is not vigour, not breadth of touch, but just lack of restraint.'

He writes to a woman writer: 'Here is my advice as a reader: when you depict sad or unlucky people, and want to touch the reader's heart, try to be colder—it gives their grief, as it were, a background, against which it stands out in greater relief. As it is, your heroes weep and you sigh. Yes, you must be cold.'

He repeats in a further letter to the same writer: 'Yes, I wrote to you once that you must be unconcerned when you write pathetic stories. And you did not understand me. You may weep and moan over your stories, you may suffer together with your heroes, but I consider one must do this so that the reader does not notice it. The more objective, the stronger will be the effect.'

'You might write a story, "The Wounded Doe,"' he writes to still another writer—also a woman. 'You remember how the huntsmen wound a doe; she looks at them with human eyes, and no one can bring himself to kill her. It's not a bad subject, but dangerous because it is difficult to avoid sentimentality—you must write it like a report, without pathetic phrases, and begin like this: "On such and such a date the huntsmen in the Daraganov forest wounded a young doe..." And if you drop a tear you will strip the subject of its severity and of everything worth attention in it.'

True to his own advice, this is how Chehov treats a death scene in the *Grasshopper* (a story about a young wife who, in her anxious concern to find new geniuses, betrayed the loyalty of her husband, only to discover on his death-bed that he, a young doctor, was the genuine genius that she had overlooked):

> Olga Ivanovna remembered her whole life with him, from beginning to end, with all its details, and suddenly understood that he was in real fact a rare and remarkable and, compared with those men that she knew, a great man. And remembering how her late father and his colleagues had treated him, she understood that they all had seen in him a coming celebrity. The walls, the ceiling, the lamp and carpet blinked at her sarcastically, as though they wanted to say: 'Missed him! Missed him!' With a sob she dashed out of the bedroom, flew past some unknown man in the drawing-room, and ran into her husband's study. He lay motionless on the Turkish divan, covered up to the waist with a blanket. His face had shrunk dreadfully, was thin and had a greyish-yellow colour, such as is never to be seen in the living; and only by his forehead, by his black brows, and by the familiar smile, could one recognize that this was Dimov. Olga Ivanovna quickly felt his breast, his forehead and hands. His breast was still warm, but his forehead and hands were unpleasantly cold. And the half-closed eyes looked, not upon Olga Ivanovna, but at the blanket.

'Dimov!' she called loudly. 'Dimov!'

She wanted to explain to him that *that* had been a mistake, that not all is lost yet, that life may be beautiful and happy still, that he is a rare, unusual—a great man, and that she will all her life cower before him, pray and feel a holy awe.

'Dimov!' she called him, shaking him by the shoulder and unable to believe that he will never wake. 'Dimov! But Dimov!'

While in the drawing-room the doctor was saying to the maid:

'What's there to ask about? You just go down to the church lodge and ask them where the pauper women live. They will wash the corpse and lay it out—do all that's necessary.'

And this is how he treats the death of a soldier on a hospital ship in the Indian Ocean [*Gusev*]:

It was stifling, one hadn't strength to breathe, one was thirsty, the water was warm, disgusting. The ship heaved as much as ever.

Suddenly something strange happened to one of the soldiers playing cards. . . He called hearts diamonds, got muddled in his score, and dropped his cards, then with a frightened, foolish smile looked round at all of them.

'I shan't be a minute, mates. I'll . . .' he said, and lay down on the floor.

Everybody was amazed. They called to him; he did not answer.

'Stepan, maybe you are feeling bad, eh?' the soldier with his arm in a sling asked him. 'Perhaps we had better fetch the priest, eh?'

'Have a drink of water, Stepan . . .' said the sailor. 'Here, lad, drink.'

'What are you knocking the mug against his teeth for?' said Gusev angrily. 'Don't you see, turnip head?'

'What?'

'What?' Gusev repeated, mimicking him. 'There's no breath in him, he's dead! That's what! What nonsensical people, God help us!'

This is how he ends another story, *Typhus*, in which a brother, on his recovery, learns of the death of his sister:

'Well, aunt,' he said joyfully. 'What has been the matter?'

'Spotted typhus.'

'Really. But now I am well, quite well! Where is Katya?'

'She is not at home. I suppose she has gone somewhere after her examination.'

The old lady said this and looked at her stocking; her lips began quivering, she turned away, and suddenly broke into sobs. Forgetting the doctor's prohibition in her despair, she said:

'Ah, Katya, Katya! Our angel is gone! Is gone!... She caught typhus from you, and is dead. She was buried the day before yesterday.'

This terrible, unexpected news was fully grasped by Klimov's consciousness; but terrible and startling as it was, it could not overcome the animal joy that filled the convalescent. He cried and laughed, and soon began scolding because they would not let him eat.

Only a week later, when, leaning on Pàvel, he went in his dressing-gown to the window, looked at the overcast sky, and listened to the unpleasant clang of the old iron rails which were being carted by, his heart ached, he burst into tears, and leaned his forehead against the window-frame.

'How miserable I am!' he muttered. 'My God, how miserable!'

And joy gave way to the boredom of everyday life and the feeling of his irrevocable loss.

Suicide is well handled in *Volodya*:

The satchel and the books lying about in the corners reminded him of the examination he had missed. . . . For some reason there came into his mind, quite inappropriately, Mentone, where he had lived with his father when he was seven years old; he thought of Biarritz and two little English girls with whom he ran about on the sand. . . He tried to recall to his memory the colour of the sky, the sea, the height of the waves, and his mood at the time, but he could not succeed. The English girls flitted before his imagination as though they were living; all the rest was a medley of images that floated away in confusion.

. . . Volodya put the muzzle of the revolver to his mouth, felt something like a trigger or spring, and pressed it with his finger... Then felt something else projecting, and once more pressed it. Taking the muzzle out of his mouth, he wiped it with the lapel of his coat, looked at the lock. He had never in his life taken a weapon in his hand before.

'I believe one ought to raise this . . .' he reflected. 'Yes, it seems so.'

Avgustin Mihailich went into the 'general room,' and with a laugh began telling them about something. Volodya put the muzzle in his mouth again, pressed it with his teeth, and pressed something with his fingers. There was a sound of a shot. . . . Something hit Volodya in the back of his head with terrible violence, and he fell on the table with his face downward among the bottles and glasses. Then he saw his father, as in Mentone, in a tall-hat with a wide black band on it, wearing mourning for some lady, suddenly seize him by both hands, and they fell headlong into a very deep, dark pit.

Then everything was blurred and vanished.

And here is a marvellous passage from *Gusev*, describing the death of a consumptive Russian soldier on a hospital ship homeward bound, and his burial at sea:

Gusev went back to the ward and got into his hammock... He dozed, and murmured in his sleep, and, worn out with nightmares, his cough, and the stifling heat, towards morning he fell into a sound sleep. He dreamed that they were just taking the bread out of the oven in the barracks and he climbed into the stove and had a steam-bath in it, lashing himself with a bunch of birch twigs. He slept for two days, and at midday on the third two sailors came down and carried him out.

He was sewn up in sailcloth, and, to make him heavier, they put with him two iron weights. Sewn up in the sailcloth he looked like a carrot or a radish: broad at the head and narrow at the feet.

Before sunset they brought him up to the deck and put him on a plank; one end of the plank lay on the side of the ship, the other on a box, placed on a stool. Round him stood the soldiers and the officers with their caps off.

There follows a description of the simple service; then:

The man on watch duty tilted up the end of the plank, Gusev slid off and flew head foremost, turned a somersault in the air and splashed into the sea. He was covered with foam and for a moment looked as though he were wrapped in lace, but the moment passed and he disappeared in the waves.

He went rapidly towards the bottom. Would he reach it? It was said to be three miles to the bottom. After sinking sixty or seventy feet, he began moving more and more slowly, swaying rhythmically, as though he were hesitating, and, carried along by the current, moved more rapidly sideways than downwards.

Then he was met by a shoal of the fish called harbour pilots. Seeing the dark body, the fish stopped as though petrified, and suddenly turned round and disappeared. In less than a minute they flew back swift as an arrow to Gusev, and began zigzagging round him in the water.

Another writer, seeing that he is about to introduce a scene of horror, would be choosing superlative adjectives adequate to the degree of terror that he is striving to express, while Chehov's artistic instinct of restraint does not desert him.

After that another dark body appeared. It was a shark. It swam under Gusev with dignity and no show of interest, as though it did not notice him, and he sank down upon its back; then it turned belly upward, basking in the warm, transparent water, and languidly opened its jaws with two rows of teeth. The harbour pilots are delighted, they stop to see what will come next. After playing a little with the body, the shark nonchalantly puts its jaws under it, cautiously touches it with its teeth, and the sailcloth is rent its full length from head to foot; one of the weights falls out and frightens the harbour pilots, and, striking the shark on the ribs, goes rapidly to the bottom.

And the story concludes :

> Overhead at this time the clouds are massed together on the side where the sun is setting ; one cloud like a triumphal arch, another like a lion, a third like a pair of scissors. . . From behind the clouds a broad, green shaft of light pierces through and stretches to the middle of the sky ; a little later another, violet-coloured, lies beside it ; next that, one of gold, then one rose-coloured. . . The sky turns a soft lilac. Looking at this gorgeous, enchanted sky, at first the ocean scowls, but soon it, too, takes tender, joyous, passionate colours for which it is hard to find a name in human speech.

The style here is so completely fitted to communicate to us the maximum impression, that Chehov himself, we feel, could not have been more acutely stirred when he conceived the subject. If (as we are made to feel) on his subsequent perusals of this tale he recaptured the self-same feeling which had urged him to the story, we may say that in this story his sensibility has communicated itself to us in perfect style.

& VIII

'Why don't I know foreign languages ?' he once wrote in a letter. (He knew French and German, but not thoroughly.) 'It seems to me I could translate magnificently. When I read anyone else's translation, I keep altering and transposing the words in my brain, and the result is something light, ethereal, like lace-work.' There is a certain distinguishable melodic strain that runs through Chehov's prose. It bursts out at intervals, but his restraint puts the brake on it each time and guides it into effective channels, and, in fact, enhances the effect of music by our sense of the restraint imposed : we are more moved because we feel the fountain of emotion behind these modest sprays. This passage from *The Kiss* is illustrative of the melody of a not infrequent emotion that, we suspect, comes to him in gushes, soaking, as it were, the story through, indeed inspiring its conception. Chehov's ideas are determined by emotion : they are emotional ideas, conveying a particular atmosphere. (This is, however, another point where much allowance should be made for the inevitable inadequacy of the translation of passages beautiful in the original.) The officer Ryabovich, in a melancholy mood, watches the river on his return to a place of romantic memory :

> The water was running, he knew not where or why, just as it did in May. In May it had flowed into the great river, from the great river into the sea ; then it had risen in vapour, turned into rain, and perhaps the very same water was running now before Ryabovich's eyes again. . . What for ? Why ?
>
> And the whole world, the whole of life, seemed to Ryabovich an unintelligible, aimless jest. . . And turning his eyes from the water and looking at the sky, he remembered again how fate in the image of an unknown woman had by chance caressed him, he remembered his summer dreams and fancies, and his life struck him as extraordinarily meagre, poverty-stricken, and colourless.

And this passage, from the *Beauties*, has almost the same melodic strain :

> And the oftener she fluttered by me with her beauty, the more acute became my sadness. I felt sorry both for her and for my-self and for the Little Russian, who mournfully watched her every time she ran through the cloud of chaff to the carts. Whether it was envy of her beauty, or that I was regretting that the girl was not mine, and never would be, or that I was a stranger to her ; or whether I vaguely felt that her rare beauty was accidental, unnecessary, and, like everything on earth, of

short duration; or whether, perhaps, my sadness was that peculiar feeling which is excited in man by the contemplation of real beauty, God only knows.

The three hours of waiting passed unnoticed. It seemed to me that I had not had time to look properly at Màsha when Karpo drove up to the river, bathed the horse, and began to put it in the shafts. The wet horse snorted with pleasure and kicked its hoofs against the shafts. Karpo shouted to it: 'Ba-ack!' My grandfather woke up. Màsha opened the creaking gates for us, we got into the chaise and drove out of the yard. We drove in silence as though we were angry with one another.

When, two or three hours later, Rostov and Nahichevan appeared in the distance, Karpo, who had been silent the whole time, looked round quickly, and said:

'A fine wench, that at the Armenian's.' And lashed his horses.

Or this beautiful ending of *The Lady with the Dog*:

Then they spent a long while taking counsel together, talked of how to avoid the necessity for secrecy, for deception, for living in different towns and not seeing each other for long at a time. How could they be free from this intolerable bondage?

'How? How?' he asked, clutching his head. 'How?'

And it seemed as though in a little while the solution would be found, and then a new and splendid life would begin; and it was clear to both of them that they had still a long, long way to go, and that the most complicated and difficult part of it was only just beginning.

& IX

But where Chehov excels himself is in the theme of farewells. He proves it in the parting scene in the third act of the *Sea-Gull*, in the last act of *Uncle Vanya*, again in the last act of the *Three Sisters*, and lastly in the final act of the *Cherry Orchard*, which is a crowning example of his delicate art of emotional orchestration. The devices to enhance the poignancy of the last scene, when brother and sister, the proprietors of the lost Cherry Orchard, fall into each other's arms and sob quietly, stealthily, afraid to be overheard, are more than ingenious, since they are also calculated to make the scene so absolutely natural that one is not aware of the psychological ingenuity behind it all till one reads the act again. And then, how one enjoys even the sheer ingenuity of this delicate emotional *ensemble*! It is difficult to resist quoting the entire act. But, to take only one thread out of a score, this is how he leads up to the final outburst of long-repressed emotion. The old Gaev thus consoles himself and the others (we feel, somewhat insincerely) for the loss of their beautiful estate, which they are now to leave within a few moments : 'Really, now everything's all right. Till the sale of the Cherry Orchard we were all of us perturbed, pained, but afterwards, when the question had been irrevocably settled, we all calmed down, felt cheerful even... I'm a bank clerk, I'm a financier now . . . and you Liuba [his sister], for whatever reason, look better, there's no doubt about it.' She says : 'Yes. My nerves are better, that's true.' She is helped on with her hat and coat. 'I sleep well. Take my things out, Yasha (*to the valet*). It's time.' But the cold indifference of these remarks serves as a relief against what is coming. As the time approaches for them to leave their home, Gaev for a moment gives vent to his sentimental nature : 'My friends, my kind, dear friends! In leaving this house for ever, can I keep silent, can I resist the desire to speak in farewell of the feelings that now engulf my whole being.' But he is cut short by the entreaties of the others to contain himself. In the meanwhile, emotion is constantly interrupted, as in real life, by preoccupations not to miss the train, not to leave something behind, and the student Trofimov cannot find his old goloshes till the very last, when they are accidentally discovered beside a trunk.

TROFIMOV. Come along, all of you, it's time we drove off!
LOPAHIN. Epihodov, my coat!
LIUBOV ANDREIEVNA. I will sit here just a moment longer. It's as though I had never seen what walls, what ceilings there are in this house, and now I look at them so greedily, with such tender love.
GAEV. I remember, when I was six years old, it was Whitsunday, as I sat on this window-sill and watched my father go to church.
LIUBOV ANDREIEVNA. Have they got all the things?

Side doors are being locked. Singly, and in pairs, they file out of the old house. Liubov Andreievna and Gaev, the last to go, linger for a moment. 'It is as though they had waited for this, they fall onto each other's neck and weep restrainedly, quietly, afraid lest they be heard.'

GAEV (*in despair*). Sister mine, sister mine.
LIUBOV ANDREIEVNA. O, my gentle, my tender, beautiful orchard!... My life, my youth, my happiness, good-bye!... Good-bye!

They are being called from outside by the others. But she cannot tear herself away: 'To look a last time at these walls, these windows... Our mother liked to walk in this room.'

GAEV. Sister mine, sister mine!

They are being called again. She calls back 'We're coming! . . .' and they, too, go out. And some little time after the sounds of the departing carriages have died away, one hears how, far away in the garden, the trees are being felled—by order of the new proprietor.

It is difficult to choose between the last two plays of Chehov. The *Cherry Orchard*, the last he wrote, and generally accepted as his masterpiece, is, as Mr. Middleton Murry aptly said, ' a shower of laughing tears,' but its plot is simple if compared to that of the *Three Sisters*, through which there runs an undercurrent of a stillness which is the very water of existence (it is not peculiar to Russia or provincial life, but may be come across in the busiest of centres, in the jolliest of lives), so that one wonders if, after all, the *Three Sisters* is not Chehov's greatest work. It is more withering, more poignantly dramatic than the *Cherry Orchard*, whose only blemish, by the way, is perhaps the introduction of the old servant at the end, whose final mutterings one would wish had been left out: there is just a touch of stage-effect in his having been locked up, by an oversight.

' O, if there were a life in which every one grew younger and more beautiful,' is a wish set down in his note-book. But that the reverse is true is at the back of all his dramas. All the time he works on real life. But in his hands it becomes more than real life; and, after Chehov has done with it, it is still real life. What he has done to it we do not know: but it has become beautifully, strangely disturbing. There is behind it all a quite exceptional gift of love and sympathy, a gift without which, one feels, the broth that is so essentially his even before he serves it out to us, would not blend or hold together. And there is that sense of the temporary nature of our existence, on this earth at all events, that he seems never able to forget, through which human beings, scenery, and even the very shallowness of things, are transfigured with a sense of disquieting importance. It is a sense of temporary possession in a temporary existence that, in the face of the unknown, we dare not undervalue. It is as if his people hastened to express their worthless individualities, since that is all they have, and were aghast that they should have so little in them to express : since the expression of it is all there is. And life is at once too long and too short to be endured.

CHAPTER FIVE

A CLOSER EXAMINATION OF PERFECTLY CHARACTERISTIC PASSAGES IN WHICH HIS SENSIBILITY IS COMPLETELY EXPRESSED

§ I

CRITICS on the look out for rough-and-ready definitions have been wont to say that Chehov was a writer who specialized in heroes of a hopeless, gloomy, and futile variety, presumably to the exclusion of such as would be deemed successes by their ability to ' get things done.' Life would be a simple matter if this indeed were the dividing-line between two camps of humanity : the successful, ' forward,' ' up-and-doing ' type, and the inert, day-dreaming, and futile. Here is an extract from Chehov's note-book—a thought that throws some light upon his attitude towards the people he depicts :

> Why do people describe only the weak, surly, and frail as sinners ? And every one when he advises others to describe only the strong, healthy, and interesting means himself.

The so-called ' failures ' he presents to us are not altogether failures : they are half-successes. They are, in fact, the self-same people who in private deem themselves successes and who do not recognize themselves because they are depicted as they seem to others, not as they see themselves. Chehov, the most balanced of modern writers, is in his attitude to the people he depicts both objective and subjective ; and that for two reasons. It is the objective way of looking at a character that really makes him live; and it is the subjective attitude which is the fair one. Fifty per cent of objectivity applied to the average mortal—and behold, the acknowledged success is fifty per cent a failure! But Chehov will grant him his due share of subjectivity to show us that, like the rest of us, he is a suffering unit.

In a letter to Suvorin he comments on an article by Merezhkovski:

> He calls me a poet, he styles my stories 'novelli' and my heroes 'failures'—that is, he follows the beaten track. It is time to give up these 'failures,' superfluous people, etc., and to think of something original. Merezhkovski calls my monk [*Easter Eve*] who composes the songs of praise a failure. But how is he a failure? God grant us all a life like his: he believed in God, and he had enough to eat and he had the gift of composing poetry. . . To divide men into the successful and the unsuccessful is to look at human nature from a narrow, preconceived point of view. Are you a success or not? Am I? Is Napoleon? Is your servant Vasili? What is the criterion? One must be a god to be able to tell successes from failures without making a mistake.

It is, no doubt, convenient to hang upon a writer of whom one knows little some such label as, for example, that Dostoevski is the exponent of the philosophy of suffering, Tolstoy of that of non-resistance to evil, and Chehov of futility. These remarks are trite, and they have just a grain of truth in them; but if they are concise, they are also negligible. The choice of really ineffectual people is in fact rare in Chehov, and, when it happens, is occasioned by the comic possibilities inherent in them. The old doctor in the *Three Sisters* who had forgotten the little he ever knew of medicine, or the helpless Gaev in the *Cherry Orchard*, are exceptions, and as such can be found in the literature and community of any country. Perhaps, on the whole, Westerners are not inclined to let themselves go quite so easily as some Russians are. Their inhibitions are quite properly allied with their sense of self-preservation. And there is still a fairly prevalent Russian type exponential of its 'broad Russian nature' to which inhibition means nothing more than cowardice. But this gives no ground for generalization. One need only read Mr. George Moore's *In Single Strictness* to realize that the so-called 'Chehovian' type is not confined to Russia. The only pity is that Mr. Moore has not the gift of humour to portray the subject as it really ought to be portrayed—by blending pathos with humour. All we are given is pathos; and we are left with an unpleasant taste in our mouth, as if we had tasted of an over-seasoned dish, because a necessary ingredient has been omitted. Indubitably the fault of the cook!

Chehov's mind is a search-light cast, not upon the weaklings of society, but upon the average citizen of town and country who, if he saw himself in this clear light, would be astonished and amused at the comi-tragedy of his self-sufficiency. But people rarely see themselves in this strong light, because their individual visions of themselves are distorted by the perspective of looking to the future with expectancy and hope. They know little of how they look against the background of surrounding life. That withering touch which is so sensible through Chehov's pages comes from seeing life that is at the moment being lived, from the other end, as if it had been lived already: for all along we had been made to guess how inevitably it *will* be lived; and in this cold transparent light we see the living hopes as cherished foibles, and the hopes that are to those who hope them sufficient and sustaining blight us by the knowledge of their impending bankruptcy. We are aghast by the spectacle of thwarted life trudging blindly to its near-by grave, terrified by the wonted insufficiency of other people's self-sufficiency. It is the terror of smugness brought to bear on incomprehensible life.

In *Three Years* a very ordinary woman, dying after a life of very ordinary happenings, says to her more than ordinary brother: 'What a good man you are! What a clever man!' This expression of affection hangs in mid-air, as something almost trite let loose into a universe mysterious with the awe and wonder surrounding those human envelopes, who utter what they feel about the life that bore them and in which—to what purpose?—they are again dissolved like empty sounds. Contrariwise, there runs the alternative suspicion that if this love be all in a universe of void, then it is 'the one gleam of spirit in all the windy vastness of a dead and empty universe.' A sense of possible alternative is just what lends his work a balance of quiet optimism which reconciles him, smilingly, with the inevitable. It then means that the Darling, however poor in mind, is rich in kindliness and love, and that if this love be the beginning of a cultural tradition that, centuries ahead, is to develop in mankind the spirit we call God, as yet only anticipated, then the Darling and her kind are the peaks of life.

This 'double' atmosphere we find in *Ariadna*, the *Black Monk*, *The Wife*, *Ward No.* 6, *A Dreary Story*, and many others, but nowhere more, perhaps, than in *Three Years*. It is obtained, as I have shown, through an objective treatment of subjectivity—to borrow the language of critics! We are made to feel that, while each individual lives an imagined and therefore, to him, a more laudable life because he builds upon the future and the past while perennially inclined to overlook ugly, trifling, irritating incongruities of the present as temporary and irrelevant things, his fellow-creatures' vision of him is the reverse side of the coin: the irrelevancies of everyday life stand out while his dream is smiled at. It comes to this: life cannot be experienced to the brim other than by way of self-sufficiency; but once the vessel is full, the lid must come off to let in fresh air, or we suffocate. Mystery is the fresh air; discontent, the safety-valve. The hero of *Three Years* found that marriage to a beautiful wife who did not love him was not unmitigated bliss as he had imagined when he had first proposed to her. Afterwards he came to the conclusion that the peak of happiness for him was really when as a young man he had found that she had left her parasol in his sister's house and he had sat up all night with it, because he was in love. Three years after they had been married she began to love him, but now it did not move him as he had thought it would.

> She stood up and passed her hand over his hair, and scanned his face, his shoulders, his hat, with interest.
>
> 'You know I love you,' she said, and flushed crimson. 'You are precious to me. Here you've come. I see you, and I'm so happy I can't tell you. Well, let us talk. Tell me something.'
>
> She had told him she loved him, and he could only feel as though he had been married to her for ten years, and that he was hungry for his lunch.

And when he met the children—his nieces—he thought: 'How they have grown! What changes in the last three years... But one might have, perhaps, to live another thirteen, thirty years... What awaits us still in the future! Live—and see.' He embraced his nieces and said to them: 'Grandpapa sends his love... Uncle Fyodor is dying. Uncle Kostia has sent a letter from America and sends you his love in it. He's bored at the exhibition and will soon be back. And Uncle Alyosha [i.e. himself] is hungry.' The story ends on a note cumulative of the tone that was designed to lead up to it:

> And when they lunched on the terrace, Yartsev [a friend] smiled somehow gladly and bashfully and all the time looked at Julia, at her beautiful neck. Laptev [the husband] watched him involuntarily, and thought that perhaps one might have to live another thirteen, thirty years. . . And what would one have to go through in that time? What awaits us in the future?
>
> And thought:
>
> 'Live—and see.'

We cannot fail to notice the emotional significance of Chehov's deliberate enumeration of such seemingly casual trivialities as that, while one man is dying and another sends his love and is bored at an exhibition, a third is hungry for his lunch; that while a friend is gazing rapturously at the lovely woman for whom her husband three years ago had felt an unrequited love, and whom she has just begun to love, the husband now can only feel as if he had been married to her for ten years, and that it might be necessary, perhaps, to live another thirteen, thirty years—which he neither looks forward to, nor yet particularly objects to. He has exhausted his self-sufficiency; and now the lid is off, but he has not yet begun to inhale new mysteries. We catch him at the end in an uninspired mood when, stripped of ecstasy, the trivial things for him are yet slightly tinged with awe because there seem to be no others, and life, in all its ordinariness, seems unique.

& II

Chehov's ironic touch is tinged with melancholy, and the blend is irresistible. It is like the evening sun shining through wet foliage—beautifully, peculiarly disquieting.

Anna on the Neck is full of it. The farewell at the station; her emotions in the train as she started on the honeymoon with her old ungainly husband whom she feared; and the contrast at the end when she had learnt to get the better of him and marshalled him at her will. If ever the word 'delightful' was applicable, it is so to *Anna on the Neck*. This is how the elderly civil servant spoke to his young wife (whose name was Anna) as the train steamed out of the station on the day of their honeymoon:

> 'I cannot help remembering now one circumstance,' he said, smiling. 'When, five years ago, Kosorotov received the order of St. Anna of the second grade, and went to thank his Excellency, his Excellency expressed himself as follows: "So now you have three Annas: one in your buttonhole and two on your neck.' And it must be explained that at that time Kosorotov's wife, a quarrelsome and frivolous person, had just returned to him, and that her name was Anna. I trust that when I receive the Anna of the second grade his Excellency will not have occasion to say the same thing to me.'

We pity the young wife, who is so completely dominated by her old husband. But time goes on, there is a big dance, and through her emotions we perceive her real nature, the development of which she is capable, how she asserts herself but yet remains the trivial thing that she essentially is. At the ball:

> A huge officer in epaulettes—she had been introduced to him in Staro-Kievski Street when she was a schoolgirl, but now she could not remember his name—seemed to spring from out of the ground, begging her for a waltz, and she flew away from her husband, feeling as though she were floating away in a sailing-boat in a violent storm, while her husband was left far away on the shore.

(Notice, by the way, Chehov's uncanny way of securing the illusion of reality by such intimate retrospective details thrown in here and there, as that she had been introduced to him in a particular street, but could not remember his name.) It was her personal success at the ball that induced her revolt.

She danced the mazurka with the same huge officer ; he moved gravely, as heavily as a dead carcase in a uniform, twitched his shoulders and his chest, stamped his feet very languidly—he felt fearfully disinclined to dance. She fluttered round him, provoking him by her beauty, her bare neck ; her eyes glowed defiantly, her movements were passionate, while he became more and more indifferent, and held out his hands to her as graciously as a king.

'Bravo, bravo!' said people watching them.

But little by little the huge officer, too, broke out ; he grew lively, excited and, overcome by her fascination, was carried away and danced lightly, youthfully, while she merely moved her shoulders and looked slyly at him as though she were now the queen and he were her slave ; and at that moment it seemed to her that the whole room was looking at them. The huge officer had hardly had time to thank her for the dance, when the crowd suddenly parted and the men drew themselves up in a strange way, with their hands at their sides. His Excellency, with two stars on his dress-coat, was walking up to her. Yes, his Excellency was walking straight towards her, for he was staring directly at her with a sugary smile, while he licked his lips as he always did when he saw a pretty woman.

Her success was complete. Her Excellency, too, had noticed her, and had asked her to take part in the charity bazaar. From that evening Anna was transformed. And when her old husband, whom she had feared, and who had treated her so meanly, came to her that evening, she feared him no longer, and said to him deliberately : 'Be off, you blockhead!' From that time it was she who bullied.

She returned home every day after midnight, and went to bed on the floor in the drawing-room, and afterwards used to tell every one, touchingly, how she slept under flowers. She needed a very great deal of money, but she was no longer afraid of Modest Alexeich [her husband], and spent his money as though it were her own ; and she did not ask, did not demand it, simply sent him in the bills. ' Give bearer two hundred roubles,' or ' pay one hundred roubles at once.'

But this domestic revolution was not without its compensations for the old time-server.

At Easter, Modest Alexeich received the Anna of the second grade. When he went to offer his thanks, his Excellency put aside the paper he was reading and settled himself more comfortably in his chair.

' So now you have three Annas,' he said, scrutinizing his white hands and pink nails—' one in your buttonhole and two on your neck.'

Modest Alexeich on this point was about to make a clever joke—a play on words—and to ask his Excellency to be the sponsor for the coming Vladimir. But his Excellency merely nodded and resumed his paper.

When Nikitin [*The Teacher of Literature*] hurries home after his engagement to announce the glad news to his old colleague, who always said the obvious, his friend was sitting on the edge of the bed taking off his trousers. Nikitin stopped him, and the old man quickly pulled on his trousers and asked what was the matter, whereupon Nikitin sat down beside him on the bed and announced the news of his engagement. But all that the colleague said to it was that the girl in question had been his pupil at the high school, that she hadn't done badly in geography, but was weak in history, and, moreover, had not been attentive in the classroom.

In the story *At the Manor* there is a delightful bit of irony, when the father of two marriageable daughters, a ' feeling, tearful man,' but with a mania for malicious argument, inflicts his shockingly unwelcome views upon the desirable young man who visits them, and having done the mischief and deprived his daughters of a possible husband, sits down and writes a letter to them.

He wrote that he was already old, that no one wanted him and no one loved him, and asked his daughters to forget him and, when he dies, to bury him in a plain wooden coffin, without ceremony, or else to send his body to the hospital at Harkov for dissection. He felt that every line he wrote breathed hatred and theatricality, but could stop himself no longer, and wrote on, wrote on, wrote on.

In the *Grasshopper*, the tragedy of which depends on the woman only realizing that her husband was a man of genius when it was too late, there is a poignant passage of irony, when he comes to her to tell her, while she is dressing for the theatre, that he has grounds for thinking that the readership in general pathology is likely to be offered him :

It could be seen by his blissful, shining face that if Olga Ivanovna had shared his joy and triumph with him, he would have forgiven her all, the present and the future, and would have forgotten all, but she did not understand what was meant by a readership and by general pathology ; moreover, was afraid of being late for the theatre, and said nothing.

He sat on two minutes, smiled guiltily, and went out.

In *Three Years* the old father is described in these terms :

The old man's voice boomed unceasingly. Having nothing to do, he was laying down the law to a customer, telling him how he should order his life and his business, always holding himself up as an example. . . The old man adored himself ; from what he said it always appeared that he had made his wife and all her relatives happy, that he had been munificent to his clerks and employees, and that every one in the street and all his acquaintances should be remembering him in their prayers. Whatever he did was always right, and if things went wrong with people it was because they did not consult him; without his advice nothing could succeed. In church he always stood in front of everybody and even made remarks to the priests, if in his opinion they were not conducting the service properly, and believed that this was pleasing to God because God loved him.

As an illustration of Chehov's rapid way of getting hold of the essentials of a character, one may turn to this extract from his note-book:

X. arrived to take up duty at N.; he shows himself a despot: he is annoyed when some one else is a success; he becomes quite different in the presence of a third person; when a woman is present, his tone changes; when he pours out wine, he first puts a little in his own glass and then helps the company; when he walks with a lady, he takes her arm; in general, he tries to show refinement. He does not laugh at other people's jokes: 'You repeat yourself,' 'there is nothing new in that.' Every one is sick of him; he sermonizes. The old women nickname him 'the top.'

Or this of a wearisome woman:

'I have not read Herbert Spencer. Tell me his subjects. What does he write about?' 'I want to paint a panel for the exhibition. Suggest a subject.'

& III

It is as though Chehov were reluctant to probe too deeply in one place, for the reason that he thought that he would be wider from the mark if he did. To him truth is more as though it were a shallow thing but vast in area: hence his impartiality. But such impartiality very soon resolves itself into a curious, paradoxical stability resting, as it were, on perpetual instability at many points. He will neither assume responsibility himself nor yet fix it upon any of his people, but builds his calm upon this restless undercurrent of multitudinous people, none of whom are wholly right or wholly wrong. Sitting on this multitude of diverse folk turning round each other in their thoughts and converse, Chehov does indeed enjoy a smooth run, as he might travel on ball-bearings. For there is not a person in any of his works who could claim any sort of moral or intellectual authority for two minutes running. From the scraps of their talk that we occasionally overhear we know that they are human: that is all. It is Chehov's instinct for the truth which prompts him to make of Trofimov, the 'eternal student,' despite his initial ludicrousness, the apostle of that culture which is to culminate in the true knowledge of God. It is a characteristic touch of Chehov's that while what Trofimov says (it is in the nature of a Wells anticipation) is easily the best there is in the play in point of philosophic thought, we cannot but feel amused with Chehov that it is the slovenly 'stick-in-the-mud' Trofimov who of all men should be the one to anticipate the future happiness of man—a piece of humour of which Trofimov is, of course, unconscious. It is the man who is unable to graduate at his university who shouts with rapture, 'Forward!' Nor is the humour of it wanton. It is as likely as not that it is just the Trofimov type of man who would be best equipped to seek the truth, and the chances are that in Russia he might be a hanger-on. And again (as though in dread of generalization), Chehov sees to it that Trofimov is not represented as a common hanger-on; he lives for months on end on an estate where formerly he had been engaged as tutor: but he refuses money when it is offered him by a friendly merchant. And further still, the fact that, intellectually, he has no rivals in the *Cherry Orchard*, does not preclude Madame Ranevskaya (a reckless woman with a hazy mind) from making hay of him when, in answer to his prayer to face the truth, she says to him: 'What truth? You see where truth is, and where untruth is, but I seem to have lost my sight and see nothing. You boldly settle all important questions, but tell me, dear, isn't that because you're young, because you haven't had the time to suffer through even one of your questions?' Nor is this really final, for we hear Trofimov confess to Anya: 'Believe me, Anya, believe me! I'm not yet thirty, I'm young, I'm still a student, but I've already suffered such a lot.' And there is unconscious humour in his reference to his age, for, a moment before, this dialogue took place between him and the rich merchant Lopahin:

LOPAHIN. Our eternal student is always with the ladies.
TROFIMOV. None of your business.
LOPAHIN. He'll soon be fifty, and he's still a student.
TROFIMOV. Leave off your silly jokes!
LOPAHIN. Getting angry, eh, silly?
TROFIMOV. Shut up, can't you?

Chehov makes the old professor who is the narrator in *A Dreary Story* complain in a convincing manner of the selfishness of youth, because he has to support his officer son out of his meagre income, whereas he would rather the position were reversed. 'Apropos of that,' he writes, 'I remember also my son, the Warsaw officer. He is a clever, honest and sober man. But this is not enough for me. I think that if I had an old father, and if I knew that he had moments when he was ashamed of his poverty, I would give up my commission and would try to get a job as a plain workman.' And thus, unwittingly, the old Professor is revealing to us that he, too, is not above egoism. But he proceeds: 'Such thoughts about my children poison me. What is the good of them? To cherish an evil feeling against ordinary people because they are not heroes is only possible for a narrow and venomous man. Enough of that.' This extract shows with what an insight Chehov succeeded in getting characters to reveal themselves, even to give themselves away, but nevertheless to retain the sympathy of the reader. In *The Wife* he gets a middle-aged man to relate his own story, and narrate it pretty favourably so far as he himself is concerned; but, despite that, the reader soon perceives that he is a most trying man to live with, and that the tale is really, among other things, an unconscious explanation on the part of the narrator of the coldness and hostility which his trying personality provokes in every one with whom he comes in contact. A similar instance occurs in *The Story of an Unknown Person.* We have a specimen of irony there which, though not being really good, is yet sufficiently stimulating to be worth noting down, and while Chehov would not have used it for his own purposes—it is too cold to be really good—he yet gets a fitting character to use it to advantage. At the same time he gets another character (the narrator, who, while not conscious of his own limitations, is very conscious of the limitations of the other fellow, and particularly dislikes his horse-laughter, cold irony, and so forth) to disdain the whole performance. Orlov, the solitary young man of independent means, has been unpleasantly surprised by the sudden arrival of his mistress; and this conversation is exchanged between him and his bachelor friends:

Pekarski, continuing to profess amazement, drummed the table with his fingers, and said:

'I still don't understand you both. You're not a student and she's not a dressmaker's apprentice. You are both with means. I consider you could have hired her a separate flat.'

'No, I couldn't. You read Turgenev.'

'Why should I read him? I've already read him.'

'Turgenev in his works teaches that every lofty, honest-thinking maiden should go with the man she loves to the end of the world and serve his idea,' said Orlov, wrinkling his eyes ironically. 'The end of the world—that is *licëntia poëtica*; the whole world with all its corners is situated in the flat of the lover. Therefore not to live with the woman who loves you in the same flat means to deny her her high destiny and not to share her ideals. Yes, my dear fellow, Turgenev wrote it, and I have to eat his stew for him.'

'What's Turgenev got to do with it, I don't know,' said Gruzin softly, and shrugged his shoulders. 'But do you remember, Georges, how he walks in *The Three Encounters* late in the evening somewhere in Italy and suddenly hears: *Vieni pensando a me segretamente!*' Gruzin sang. 'Good!'

And so Chehov's calm is a deceptive calm, achieved by playing off diverse emotions and ideas (or, more properly, emotional ideas) one against the other. But that this should be so goes to the production of that artistically sublime illusion, that there is always *more* than the utmost of what he himself could possibly imply.

&IV

Chehov excels in group emotions. In his plays this is particularly noticeable. The company on the stage, as indeed in life, is to all purposes an *ensemble* of solitary souls. That no individual can wholly and continuously understand the mood of another individual at the time, because he is more particularly concerned with his own, is a favoured theme of Chehov's. When he advised writers to be cool in their presentation of emotional effects, he knew what he was doing: he wanted a contrasting background against which to reveal the more clearly the tenderness of the emotion. When, as in real life, one sensibility falls on deaf ears, that is, on a momentarily different sensibility, then they both together, or severally, shine brighter. He plays off one mood against another, and so creates a group mood —his own, which he transfers to the audience. This is one of the differences between life and art: in life the group mood is casual; in art, intentional. In Chehov it is intentionally casual; but the intention is hidden from us: this is good art. When we perceive how well it is hidden, we say: 'But this is superb art!' For it is at once like life and like art.

The old man in the *Sea-Gull* walks perpetually among the others, but is alone, as in fact each one of them is essentially alone. 'As I shall lie in the grave alone, so in fact I live alone.' He talks of wanting to go and live in town. 'Of course, it's better in town. You sit in your study, the footman lets no one in without announcing him, there's a telephone . . . cabs in the street, and all...' The doctor looks upon his craving for diversion as a triviality. And the old man answers: 'You are satiated and indifferent, and therefore have a tendency towards philosophy, while I want to live, and therefore drink wine for dinner and smoke cigars and all.' He had in his youth wanted two things; to be a writer, and to get married. But he got neither of the things he wanted, but became an 'actual states-councillor'—a rank that he never sought. The old army doctor in the *Three Sisters* complains that he never managed to get married because his life flashed by like lightning, and is answered by Andrei, who has found marriage come somewhat short of his early expectations: 'One shouldn't marry. One shouldn't, because it's dull.' Màsha, in the *Sea-Gull*, talks of her unrequited love; but nobody cares. The actress talks of her successes all through the scoring at a card-party. Nobody cares. You feel that each individual, no matter how sprightly he may be in his talk, is essentially lonely: each individual soul is three-quarters isolated. And so it is.

In what subtle emotional orchestration Chehov's sensibility manifests itself is shown by a passage like this, from the *Sea-Gull.* A mother, in a momentary flash of anger, actually resorts to the use of the very words which she had learnt only a moment since, in a casual conversation with her brother, were the most painful ones for her son to endure. He hits back, and then, suddenly, bursts into tears; and, after pacing the floor again in her excitement, she too cries, kisses him fondly, and asks him to forgive her. But when, in the effusion of emotion with which he unburdens his soul to her, he tells her that his unhappiness is mainly due to his having lost the affection of the girl he loves, she quickly tires of it. Her own lover happens to be a rival of her son with the girl in question, and he had actually challenged her lover to a duel on that account; and the mother, forgetful of her spasm of motherly love of a while ago, and unmoved by her son's love-affair, even takes this opportunity to extract a promise from him that he will not challenge her lover.

It reveals something of the instability, the flimsiness of emotion, the intertanglement of moral values, which seem like waves on the sea: now high, now low, merely of a specific, not intrinsic value. I am powerless to convey the full effect of such passages with which indeed his plays are packed—the rainbow of emotion, the waves of tears and laughter, sullenness and meanness, and sudden angers, and sudden generosities, as the people brush against each other's sensibilities with the casualness so natural of real life that it is, moreover, a sheer delight to examine his deliberate method of making it appear so. The glimpses we thus get convince us that what we see is casual, devoid of any strain of artistry. But what artistry it is to make us feel so! And when we understand the artistry our pleasure is enhanced. The glimpses are more than glimpses of what they immediately reveal: they flare up, and suddenly, as by a flash of lightning in the night, reveal the depths of human nature down to the essentials. There is a seemingly casual reference to a cab, a dog, a brooch, but suddenly the heavens are split in twain and you behold the vistas of the universe: the foundations of society shake, totter, and you see deeper into the very heart of psychological phenomena, down to the common denominator of the human soul.

'But everybody talks about our marriage,' Varya, in the *Cherry Orchard*, says to Anya, who has only just arrived with her spendthrift mother from abroad; 'everybody congratulates me, and there's nothing in it at all, it's all like a dream. (*In another tone*) You've got a brooch like a bee.' Anya answers sadly: 'Mother bought it.' Then goes into her room and talks lightly, like a child: 'In Paris I went up in a balloon!' And each of the three references sets up, for one instant only, a separate, far-reaching, emotional reality that, like a thread, goes through their lives even outside the technical compass of the play, and in the play itself is at this or other point crossed and joined by other psychological threads in the counterpoint of group emotion.

Kuligin, the self-satisfied but amiable schoolmaster in the *Three Sisters*, whose wife is gradually becoming bored with him, speaks thus:

To-day is Sunday, the day of rest, therefore let us rest, let us enjoy ourselves each according to his age and station. The carpets should be put away for the summer till winter-time. . .

Use Persian powder or naphthalin. . . The Romans were healthy because they knew how to work and how to rest; they had *mens sana in corpore sano*. Their life flowed according to certain forms. Our Headmaster says: The chief thing in life is its form. . . Whatever loses its form, ends—and in our everyday life it's the same (*takes Màsha round the waist, laughingly*). Màsha loves me. My wife loves me. And the window-blinds also, with the carpets. . . To-day I am jolly, in the best of moods. Màsha, at four o'clock we are due at the Headmaster's. There's a walk being got up for the pedagogues and their families.

MÀSHA. I'm not going.

KULIGIN (*grieved*). Dear Màsha, why not?

MÀSHA. We'll talk of it afterwards . . . (*angrily*) Very well, I'll go, only leave me alone, please . . . (*goes aside*).

KULIGIN. And then the evening we'll spend at the Headmaster's. In spite of his ill-health, this man tries above all things to be sociable. An excellent, lofty personality. A wonderful man. Yesterday, after the meeting, he says to me: 'I'm tired out, Fyodor Ilyich! Tired out!' (*looks at the clock on the wall, then at his own watch*). Your clock is seven minutes fast. Yes, he says, I am tired out!

This little passage alone reveals the comi-tragedy of their relations, as his wife's boredom is thrown up into relief by the schoolmaster's complacency and dullness. Nor is the fact of his sympathy for his chief lost sight of: we learn afterwards, casually of course, that the schoolmaster, if no one else in the group, 'gets on.' There is something merciless and blindly cruel in people's misunderstandings of their fellows' sensibilities which Chehov never loses sight of.

&V

By a few strokes Chehov manages to make his people live. This is how, in the course of two sentences, he makes us visualize the little boy in *The Darling*:

The veterinary's wife arrived—a thin, plain lady, with short hair and a peevish expression. With her was her little Sasha, a boy of ten, small for his age, blue-eyed, chubby, with dimples in his cheeks. And scarcely had the boy walked into the yard when he ran after the cat, and at once there was the sound of his gay, joyous laugh.

It is touches like this, strokes of this kind, that get at the heart of a character. In *The Steppe* there is an equally delightful picture of a little boy arriving at a strange house where he is henceforth to live; and in one or two sentences the scene is made more true than life itself. The little boy sits at a table with his hostess, who sews and keeps on dropping her thimble under the table, whereupon her little daughter crawls down to get it for her and each time remains for long under the table to examine with curiosity the legs of the little new arrival. In *Anna on the Neck* the character of the old husband is amplified by such strokes as this. In a theatre, during the interval, his young wife on his arm, he would stroll up to the refreshment bar, squeeze a pear in his hand, and having asked the price of it, say 'Indeed?' and put it back again.

Nor must the Darling with her affection for the little boy she has adopted be overlooked. This is the story which Tolstoy confessed he could not read without tears.

Olenka talked to him and gave him tea. Her heart warmed, and there was a sweet ache in her bosom, as though the boy had been her own child.

She who had in turn been interested only in the profession of her first husband, then only in that of her second, always to the exclusion of all else, would now talk of nothing but what related to the little boy; and when she went to the market she would talk of how difficult it was nowadays for little boys at school, and how exigent the teachers had become, and so on.

Then he would go down the street to school, a little figure, wearing a big cap and carrying a satchel on his shoulder. Olenka would follow him noiselessly.

'Sashenka!' she would call after him, and she would pop into his hand a date or a caramel. When he reached the street where the school was, he would feel ashamed of being followed by a tall, stout woman; he would turn round and say:

'You'd better go home, auntie. I can go the rest of the way alone.'

The story ends on the same touchingly delightful note:

At three o'clock they had dinner together; in the evening they learned their lessons together and cried. When she put him to bed, she would stay a long time making the sign of the cross over him and murmuring a prayer; then she would go to bed and dream of that far-away misty future when Sasha would finish his studies and become a doctor or an engineer, would have a big house of his own with horses and a carriage, would get married and have children. . . She would fall asleep still thinking of the same thing, and tears would run down her cheeks from her closed eyes, while the black cat lay purring beside her, 'Mrr, mrr, mrr.'

And this is the concluding sentence:

She would go back to bed thinking of Sasha, who lay sound asleep in the next room, sometimes crying out in his sleep:

'I'll give it you! Get away! Shut up!'

The temptation to quote grows irresistible as I write. This is the worst of writing about Chehov: he has an inexhaustible fund of particular delights, and one would fain quote them all. Examples will not do justice to him. To schedule them would appear a painful process. Perhaps critical studies should not be written. It appals me to think of what I have left untouched. I have said next to nothing of that masterpiece, *A Dreary Story*, written at the age of twenty-nine. There is in it a mood—the indirect communication of a particularly deadly kind of anxiety to two other human beings at a distance—a piece of psychology beautifully handled. I have said nothing of the nervous, tragic atmosphere in *The Story of an Unknown Person*, as the pseudo-valet, with his head still wet from the snow—he had run out into the street bareheaded—rushes back to his room and ponders upon his departure. 'The large windows with the dark curtains, the bed, the crumpled dress-coat on the floor, and the wet footprints from my boots, looked at me sternly and sadly. And the stillness was a peculiar one.' Nor have I mentioned his mood in Venice during convalescence.—But let me better pass on to the last section of this essay—Chehov's thematic method of construction.

& VI

His works are built up as though they were Wagnerian operas—on *Leitmotifs*. These themes are principally determined by the fact that each character in Chehov is, as I have said, an isolated soul that, in essentials, lives alone in a world of its own creation through which it looks upon the life 'that is' in a misty, half-uncomprehending way; and the blend, the clash, the incongruity of it is what moves us: there is beauty in that blend of comicality and pathos. There is Madame Ranevskaya, the owner of the Cherry Orchard, who has a world of her own—one can feel it plainly throughout the play—and only every now and then she comes down to earth to face reality, but not for long. And there is Anya, her daughter of seventeen, who also has her world and her 'new life'; and there is the poor 'eternal student,' who lives mostly outside the present. And what each thinks about he lets out inadvertently between relevant sentences in the colloquial way, and—strangely—it so happens that what matters to him most is to appear irrelevant to the company in which he lives. In the *Sea-Gull* the young teacher always broods over his poverty and the fact that he has to keep a family on twenty-three roubles a month, while the estate-agent is always lost in reminiscence of theatrical news of the past generation. Thus, when the estate-agent relates how a famous bass, Silva, once took the low C, and a church cantor in the gallery consternated every one by booming out 'Bravo, Silva!' a whole octave lower, the teacher only asks: 'And what is the pay of a church cantor?'

The thematic construction is nowhere more apparent than in his plays. There is the young doctor's theme in *Uncle Vanya*, 'Those who will live one or two hundred years after us.' This is how he puts it in the course of a narration in the first act when he relates how a patient died before him under chloroform: 'I sat down, closed my eyes—like that, and thought: those who will live one or two hundred years after us, and for whom we are now treading the path, will they remember us gratefully?' He takes up the theme again in the fourth act, thus: 'Those who will live one or two hundred years after us, and who will despise us for having lived our lives so stupidly and so tastelessly—they may perhaps find the means to be happy, but we. . . You and I have but one hope. The hope that when we shall sleep in our graves, we shall see visions, perhaps even pleasant ones.' And at the conclusion of the play Sonia takes up a theme which may, in part, be said to flow out of the theme I have quoted: '. . . and there, beyond the grave, we shall say that we had suffered, that we had cried, that our lot had been bitter, and God will take pity on us, and both of us, uncle, dear uncle, shall see a life lofty and tender and beautiful, we shall know gladness and look on our present predicaments with affection, a smile—and we shall rest.' It runs on: 'We shall rest! We shall hear angels, we shall see heaven all diamonds, we shall see how all evil drowns in the mercy that shall engulf the whole world, and our life will be peaceful and tender and sweet, like a caress...'

This passage is strikingly beautiful in the original. And it is interesting to note here that the particular element which lends it (and the final passages in the *Three Sisters*) its peculiar, disturbing beauty is perhaps the inadequacy, almost falseness, of the consolation. In the final passages of the *Three Sisters* that particular emotional effect is even more crushing because, whereas Sonia, in *Uncle Vanya*, for the moment is really fervent about the things which are to make up for her thwarted life, the three sisters are not so sure of their consolations: hence the more disquieting effect of Olga's final speech in the *Three Sisters*—to which, however, I shall presently return. But there is, of course, an alternative (or even a simultaneous) interpretation of the final passage from *Uncle Vanya*, since Chehov never disclaimed the possibility of immortality for the individual soul, if only as part of the 'world soul,' or something of that sort, something necessarily vague, of course. Chehov's attitude was that he did not know one way or the other, but that he suspected that there may be a way which, by our present standards of logic, was neither one way nor the other, but somehow utterly another. Was it Ibsen who said that one can believe and doubt at the same time? At worst, extinction itself was a sort of bliss.

In the *Sea-Gull* Màsha's mother complains to Doctor Dorn, with whom she is in love, I think in the first or second act: 'Our time is passing.' In the third act, when she assists at the departure of the great actress and is reproved by her for crying, she answers: 'Our time is passing.' She takes a pathetic view of love; hence her tender solicitude over her daughter's unrequited love. The schoolmaster's theme in the *Three Sisters* relates to the headmaster's character, and he seems to be so concerned about his chief throughout the three preceding acts that one is not surprised to learn in the course of the last act that he has been promoted to the position of assistant headmaster. One is reminded at intervals that Solëni does not forget, even if we do, that he is like Lermontov, by his quotations from the poet. The old doctor's theme is that 'perhaps we only think that we exist, when actually we don't,' and that nothing matters. He shakes his head and mutters: 'It doesn't matter! It doesn't matter!' And there is the old deaf messenger who comes round at intervals with documents to sign and is ever waved aside by Andrei, whereupon he complains at last: 'That's what documents are for, to be signed.' He comes on again later and pleads: 'Andrei Sergeievich, it isn't as if the documents were mine, they are official. I didn't make them.' To which Andrei replies by a long soliloquy: 'Oh, what has become of my past, and where is it?' and so forth in this strain, till he concludes with a question addressed sharply to the waiting messenger: 'What do you want?' 'What? Documents want signing,' says the deaf old man. And this is answered with: 'I'm tired of you.' The play concludes with the documents still unsigned.

Irina has her 'beautiful thoughts'; Moscow is the pivot on which her existence turns. The curtain falls on her in the second act as she wails all alone in her misery: 'To Moscow! To Moscow! To Moscow!' And towards the end of the third act she tells her sister Olga that she had been always waiting till they should be settled in Moscow, where her real life would begin. She implores her sisters to go to Moscow, where they had lived as children before their late father, a general, had settled in the provinces. But they never get to Moscow, and one knows beforehand that, even if they did, it would be no solution of their essential problem. Nor is the reason why they cannot get off to Moscow by any means insurmountable: it is simply that for a thousand minor reasons they cannot get themselves to go there. One of the reasons is that their beloved brother Andrei is contemplating becoming a professor at the University of Moscow, and their plan is to remove to Moscow when the time comes for Andrei to hold the chair. But in the course of years Andrei falls in love with a local provincial girl, who, when he marries her, usurps the place of mistress of the household; and under the influence of provincial slackness he gradually abandons his professorial ambitions and takes up municipal duties, which largely consist of signing the documents that the deaf old messenger brings to his house. And as the years advance Andrei takes firmer root in the provincial town, and, like him, his fascinating but now gradually withering three sisters take up uncongenial work, and as they are growing older, provincial life is gradually drying them up, and they will, despite their fading hopes, perish slowly where they are. Yet they are all remarkable and singularly fascinating women, who should have been destined to lead more interesting lives. The drama is that the people in this play go through their lives hesitating, conscious of its shortness and its consequent lost opportunities. For some of them it has already 'flashed by like lightning,' and they are full of regrets for the things they have left undone, and those who are in their full bloom are too wise, too sensitive, too apprehensive not to be aware that a similar fate awaits them: they are wretched because they are not doing things, not living fully, while life is passing by, and they cannot make up their mind 'to live' for fear that their choice, which in the nature of things must needs exclude alternatives, may not be the real important one after all: they can do nothing because there are too many things that they could do. It would be better for them if they were dull and stupid; but they are represented to be the 'feeler' of creative evolution. They are types and individuals at the same time. They tell a friend that their knowledge of foreign languages, for example, is a useless luxury in their provincial town, and are answered by the philosophically minded Colonel Vershinin that there is not a town, however dull, where an educated person is not an asset. 'Let us assume,' he tells them, 'that among the one hundred thousand people of this coarse and backward town there are only three like you. Naturally, you will not conquer the dark mass which surrounds you; in the course of your life, little by little, you will have to give way and lose yourselves in the crowd, life will stifle you, but still you won't have vanished, won't have gone without leaving a trace; after you there might come already six like yourselves, then twelve, and so on, until, finally, people like you will prevail.' And as the play unfolds one is made aware how gradually and very slowly their lives have been changing; the progress of their years alone has been swift, the change in them has been infinitesimal. There is a tragic beauty about the three sisters, for they are too fine, too exquisitely sensitive for personal happiness. They go on working humbly, teaching with success, serving the purpose of the future happiness of mankind as much as lies in them to serve, and destined to die with their longings unsatisfied.

Throughout there runs Colonel Vershinin's theme: 'In two or three hundred years' time life on this earth will be unimaginably beautiful and wonderful,' and so on. This *motif* is first sounded by him soon after his appearance in the first act, and then recurs through all the succeeding three acts of the drama. In the second act he says: 'Well, if we can't have any tea, let's philosophize, at any rate... Let us meditate . . . about life as it will be after our time,' and so on. In the third act he comments on the effect of the fire that has broken out in the town: 'I thought that something of the sort used to happen many years ago when an enemy made a sudden attack, and looted, and burned... And at the same time what a difference there really is between the present and the past! And when a little more time has gone by, in two or three hundred years, perhaps, people will look at our present life with just the same fear, and the same contempt, and the whole past will seem clumsy and dull, and very uncomfortable, and strange. Oh, indeed, what a life there will be, what a life! . . . There are only three persons like you in the town just now, but in future generations there will be more and more, and still more, and the time will come when everything will change and become as you would have it, people will live as you do, and then you too will go out of date; people will be born who are better than you.'

Contrariwise to this, as if following the rule of counterpoint, there runs the theme of Baron Tusenbach: 'After our time people will fly about in balloons, the cut of one's coat will change, perhaps they'll discover a sixth sense and develop it, but life will remain the same, laborious, mysterious, and happy. And in a thousand years' time people will still be sighing: " Life is hard! " and at the same time they'll be just as afraid of death, and unwilling to meet it, as we are.'

In the first act Màsha says about her dead mother: 'Do you know, I'm beginning to forget her face. We'll be forgotten in just the same way.' And Colonel Vershinin replies: 'Yes, they'll forget us. It's our fate, it can't be helped. A time will come when everything that seems serious, significant, or very important to us, will be forgotten, or considered trivial.' A little later Irina says to Baron Tusenbach: 'You say that life is beautiful. Yes, but if it only seems so! The life of us three hasn't been beautiful yet; it has been stifling us as if it were weeds.' Towards the end of the third act Irina sobs: 'Where? Where has everything gone? Where is it all? O, my God, my God! I've forgotten everything, everything. . . I don't remember what is the Italian for window or, well—for ceiling. . . I forget everything, every day I forget it, and life passes and will never return, and we'll never go away to Moscow. . . I see that we'll never go. . . I'm already twenty-three, I've been at work for a long while, and my brain has dried up, and I've grown thinner, plainer, older, and there is no relief of any sort, and time goes and it seems all the while as if I were going away from the real, the beautiful life, farther and farther away, down some precipice. I'm in despair, and I can't understand how it is that I am still alive, that I haven't killed myself.'

This is, I need hardly say, the embryo of the theme that cumulates in a kind of stifled paroxysm which, by reason of the restraint placed on the emotions, is enhanced tenfold, indeed carried to the highest pitch and made wellnigh intolerable in the concluding passages, as the receding sounds of the military bands convey to our mind the marching off of the artillery brigade, and the three sisters, over-sensitive for their surroundings, find themselves alone once more. And though the brigade which is now departing to the strains of military music had caused no solution of their intimate problems, and though the presence of the officers who have bidden farewell to them had settled nothing, and such incidents as the fire that had broken out one night had only caused them to sit up till dawn, so serving as a background against which the better to set off their several emotions, yet, now that the last distraction has gone with the departed regiment, the climax is achieved. Even the news of the Baron's death in the duel is no real surprise to them; it is only in keeping with the unavailing nature of their plans; now they will certainly never go to Moscow.

It is a day of late autumn; the air is transparent and the outline of trees in the garden is sharp. The sky is pale, with a warning of winter, but it is not yet cold. The three sisters are standing on the open terrace, pressing against each other.

MÀSHA. O, how the music plays! They are leaving us, one has quite left us, quite and for ever. We remain alone, to begin our life over again. We must live . . . we must live . . .

IRINA (*puts her head on Olga's bosom*). A time will come when every one will know what all this is about, what all this suffering is for, there will be no more mysteries, but meanwhile we must live . . . work, only work! To-morrow I will go away alone, I shall teach at the school and give my whole life to those who may want it. Now it's autumn, it will soon be winter, the snow will cover everything, and I shall be working, I shall be working. . .

The emotion that has by now accumulated would be enough to overwhelm mountains. But Chehov was not an artist for nothing : in the few simple, colloquial sentences that follow, wherein, as in all great art, the particular is identified with the universal, there is compressed such stifling intensity of yearning that in a spiritual sense we gasp for breath. Here is your ' " trigger " process, the release of enormous forces by some tiny movement ':

OLGA (*embracing both sisters*). The bands are playing so gaily, so bravely, and one longs to live. Goodness . . . goodness ! Time will pass on, and we shall go away for ever ; they will forget us, forget our faces, voices, and how many there were of us. . .

Granted they recognize the purpose of ' modern culture ' that is to culminate in the clear knowledge of the spirit of God some day, but not yet awhile, are they not to be allowed a sigh for their individual soul if it is to perish on the threshold of a kingdom wherein they shall have no part : are they not to be allowed a doubt—to kindle their faith, as a draught kindles a fire ? Faith and doubt lie beyond each other—on whichever note you choose to end your little sermon. But here, too, Chehov goes one step further, and blends the note of race-hopefulness with a kind of personal weariness. The passage runs on, the intensity of yearning gaining in contrast by the ineffectual meekness of the consolation :

. . . but our suffering will turn to joy for those who will live after us, peace and happiness will reign on earth, and they will remember us with kindly sayings and bless those who are living now. O, dear sisters, our life isn't over yet. Let us live ! The bands are playing so gaily, so gladly, and it seems that in another little while we shall know why we are alive, why it is we have to suffer. . . If only one knew, if only one knew !

We are living on a higher plane; the atmosphere, as if before a thunderstorm, is charged with universal omen.

Yet Chehov, true to life, does not allow them to hold forth from the house-top: the three sisters speak half-audibly, as if each spoke to herself, and the other people present act in contrasting mood. Only a few moments earlier the old army doctor Chebutikin had been singing softly to himself the well-worn refrain, 'Ta-ra-ra-boom-de-ay; this is our washing day'—a trashy tune; which only throws into relief the mood of the three sisters, the most searching of which the human heart is capable. The music the while has been growing fainter and fainter. The dull, complacent schoolmaster, who told Irina that her wish to lose herself in public work was 'something not serious,' and who boasted that he had got on because, unlike most people, he was intelligent, now brings out the hat and coat for his despondent wife Màsha; they are going home, and he is smiling happily. Andrei, the would-be professor, wheels out the perambulator with the baby.

CHEBUTIKIN (*sings softly*). Ta-ra-ra-boom-de-ay . . . this is our washing day . . . (*reads his paper*). It doesn't matter. It doesn't matter.

OLGA. If only one knew, if only one knew!

CURTAIN

AUTHOR'S EPILOGUE

'The theatre has inflicted on me a bitter injury.' This is the epitome of Chehov. Stanislavsky drilled his actors out of sensibility into coma. Himself, he lacked Chopin's *rubato*. A book called *My Life in Art* would have struck ribaldry in any other profession. It palsied theatreland into reverence. The acute lacuna of that shattering scene in the original stage-directions, before Stanislavsky cut it out, when the baron killed in the duel is brought in on a stretcher, should now be restored, as Chehov wanted it.

So should Masha's thematic closing speech about migrant birds, whose vision God hath opened. 'Darling,' his wife wrote to him at Nice, 'those lines are rather a mouthful.' And, like a lamb, he cut them out, though really she was cutting his throat. He was too ill to care.

But here is some close detective work. I have traced the master's widow to Mikhail Bulgakov's satire on the Moscow Art Theatre in the person of the ageing actress Ludmilla Silvestrovna Pryakhina. Her surname disguises the too obvious Lyakhina—a Pole for a Czech. And her patronymic recalls her own—Olga Leonardovna.

William Gerhardie

1973

MY LITERARY CREDO

The practice as a profession, however precarious, of the art in which one finds one's deepest fulfilment is a happiness—in so far as the denial of it would be a misery. And misery, as Coleridge says somewhere, is not an exportable commodity, the market being everywhere glutted. As a labour of love writing is about as pleasant—conditions of authorship being what they are—as a premature childbirth in *Mother India*.

The Law of Artistic Survival

Well? Why write? Poetry being a realization of the spiritual riches subsisting under the surface of Time, of beauty present *sub specie aeternitatis* in all life, poetry is a prerequisite of happiness—a necessity. One often hears people speculating as to the chances of this or that work surviving. There are ups and downs in posthumous reputations as in everything else; but the infallible condition ensuring the survival of a book, a chapter, a character, a line, is the invocation of 'the pleasure which there is in life itself,' as Wordsworth has it—that residuum of happiness, barely noticed in the stress of living, perhaps best defined as the poetry of life. The writer has, without curbing its flight, perpetuated a moment of Time on the wing—and poetry is born. It is, after all, the fleeting that eternity is in love with; for she has no cause to be in love with the permanent: herself. If there were no such thing as time, she would have only still-life to eternize, and writers having no better claim to call themselves poets than that they do not write prose would perpetuate—as they already do—a state of coma.

The novel, the newest, the most fluid, plastic, malleable and commodious of the arts, is the rightful heir of the poem.

Why I am a Novelist

When I speak of poetry I mean, of course, writing which is not affected by that most unreal of all divisions in literature, into prose and verse. Unlike long verse—a hurdle-race over self-imposed obstacles—the novel is a bourne of unlimited horizons, peopled with living beings as symbols of poetic truth: not an excuse for putting you through a stiff exercise of rhyme and metre to see who of you can keep it up. Stendhal spoke of 'la poésie avec ses comparaisons obligées.' Again, unlike short broken-backed verse (peddling frustration dressed up as a puzzle to baffle others in addition to oneself), the novel is a diamond-shaped jewel throwing back the light it has absorbed from life: not a yard of prose sliced up into unequal lengths and passed off as a poem. If most novels are none of these things, it is not the fault of the novel but the novelist. And whether fiction or verse has contributed the larger number of still-born offspring is debatable and irrelevant to the potential advantages enjoyed by the novel as a poetic art-form most suitable to the spirit of the age. The popular distinction between the poem and the novel misses the poetic criterion—'the pleasure which there is in life itself'—common to both forms. But, unlike the poem, the novel both reproduces and elucidates the nature of this happiness.

Again, the popular distinction between light and serious reading is not a serious distinction. A woman reader, asked whether she would rather read my novel *Of Mortal Love* or my historical biography *The Romanovs*, replied: 'I am *ashamed* to say that I would prefer the novel. But my husband, who reads only serious books, would, of course, choose the biography.' Popularly, seriousness

What is Serious

is associated with a work conveying information, which the reader, in his avidity for prestige-values, confuses with knowledge. In reality, knowledge is serious when it is a revelation—a revelation of our common being moved to obey the unknown laws of the kingdom of heaven within us. Personal bias is a defect almost inseparable from the interpretation of actual events; but a work of art subordinates the ego to the higher judgment of the contemplating soul, itself constituted like a work of art and presented by the poet with an image of the world in unison with her own equations, akin to her own coherence, moving in obedience to her own laws.

In this way a work of art reveals the ineffable nature of our inner being—a form of knowledge unobtainable on a merely intellectual level. Such knowledge is in fact a religious experience, convincing as it does the reader that the visible world is not a self-contained universe but a dominion of a higher world to which it owes allegiance. But why, it may be asked, is knowledge of this order communicable through poetry and art, and not through works commonly deemed to be 'serious'—works disseminating information? The answer is, that knowledge of the higher spiritual order is impervious to the rational trick of drawing inferences from assumptions based on one's own limitations. It is communicable but inexplicable. The spiritual intelligence at the approach of the less spiritual and more material inquirer is like an aristocrat, confronted by social climbers, ignoring their company in modest and delicate shyness; or a dramatist paralysed in his attempt, foredoomed and moreover despised by his interlocutor gifted with a strong mental grip on pounds, shillings and pence, to explain to him in the same terms the working of the dénouement. The lower order of intelligence cannot see *why*, because it does not know *what*, it is incapable of comprehending. The spiritual habit, on the contrary, is to infer from our common demonstrable limitations the assumption of a reality outstripping our comprehension which ever stands in inverse ratio to our presumption. There is no defining the higher worlds. Any attempt at explicitness must result in distortion; at completeness, in ignorance of

In Inverse Ratio

what is left out. But the poet is not concerned with external and explicit, but with internal and implicit, evidence. He is a poet in consequence of his conviction, susceptible of spiritual and not material proof, that life as we know it is only half the story ; that it is but a distorted, partial image of the unknown whole of which man is the true citizen, carrying the principles of the unknown laws within himself 'without knowing who decreed that they should be.'

This view might sound dogmatic to those who assume, and assume mistakenly, that a place of honour is thereby assigned to 'serious' subjects expressing lofty, solemn and sonorous sentiments, betraying an unhealthy preoccupation with the other world to the exclusion of common everyday matters. The truth, in fact, is exactly the reverse. The more deeply rooted in life, the more steeped in humorous tragedy (that very adult compound of pathos and humour: the very spirit of an age which has outgrown Greek tragedy), the more serious in the real sense will be the work by the heavenly forces released in implication. And the more high-falutin the subject, the more grandiloquent the manner and dead-earnest the aim, the more nebulous, windy, dogmatic, flat, inaccurate, woolly, lifeless, trivial, shallow and worthless will be the result: because the writer has seen fit to use his own foolish tongue to state that which a wiser man would have left implied. No *intellectual* belief is required from the pure poet. He may, for all the difference it makes to his poetry, be a sceptic, an agnostic, an atheist, a black pessimist, a God-hater writhing in the depths of despair, or a full-throated rhapsodist singing the praises of the Lord. So long as, in his revulsion from life, in his delight in it, he has, wilfully or unwittingly, dwelt on the *strangeness* of this half-world, actual but not real, abstract but not ideal, he will have thrown into relief the missing balance, the unimaginable equation made conspicuous by its absence, the unseen half, real but not actual, ideal but

This Half-World

not abstract, together completing a world which is whole. And the miracle of pure poetry will have been achieved.

Imaginative v. Imaginary

Also, to the extent to which the texture of the novel is composed of 'emotion recollected in tranquillity,' the novel is poetic and on a higher plane of seriousness than the biography, in which the writer is debarred from recollecting his hero's emotion—in tranquillity or otherwise. Should he, in a desperate attempt to raise his biography to the imaginative level of the novel, fall back on the recollection of his own emotion, he would present the reader with emotions which, while being commendably imaginative, were also scandalously imaginary. The emotion, the poetry, in a biography, is seen from outside and is as personal to the biographer as are interpretation and conjecture. But as *Wahrheit* made fragrant by *Dichtung*, the novel is a distillation of experience. It is something intimate, yet general, secreting and reflecting in a ceaseless interplay of rays the love of a vocation and the love of life. It is a sifting out of gravel from gold dust: the passing of personal memories through the filter of time.

As an art-form the novel is unmatched in scope for revealing, while concealing in the anonymity of the third person singular, humiliating experiences which writers would shrink from confessing openly in their autobiographies. 'Fiction,' says Thackeray, 'carries a greater amount of truth in solution than the volume which purports to be all true.' And yet in the space allotted to reviews the works dangle like sausages on a string, while books about the men who wrote the works are accorded pride of place; so arguing a preference for fiction blatantly disguised as nothing-but-the-truth rather than for truth in solution modestly disguised as fiction.

The quality of truth, whether in lump or solution, varies according to the order of intellectual integrity. But there is an integrity devoid of interest, save to readers devoid of intellect. The abounding transparency of the average popular novel reduces a commonplace experience to an obvious statement, and is for those to whom the commonplace is novel, and the obvious food for thought. Conversely, the more profound and subtle and highly organized a work, the poorer the impression gained on a first reading. For the hallmark of a genuine work of literature is that it gains on further acquaintance; that it can be dipped into and enjoyed out of context; and that, as with symphonic music, the memory of its design is a prerequisite of delighted recognition of the cunning of its parts and of passionate concurrence in the cumulative fitness of the whole. 'Nothing,' Coleridge states, 'can permanently please which does not contain in itself the reason why it is so, and not otherwise.' And that needs finding out.

The Hallmark

For this reason, the more ostensibly simple but profoundly subtle the work the less likely it is to be received with immediate acclamation by critics, themselves often busy writers with their own books in arrears and old scores to pay off and wearily reviewing their fellow-craftsmen's books on a basis of Earn as You Write. Rather than sound the totality of a work by testing it as one might test a gong, the reviewer, sooner than attempt to define the nature of your talent (which would require exercising his own talent), will pick on some subordinate thought or quarrel with your facts, and, casting doubts on your veracity, dismiss your work from his mind, and the reader's.

Reviewers

The self-confident writer, it is generally thought, cares nothing for the reviewer's opinion. And, in truth, the worse the opinion the less he thinks of his critic: but the more he resents his opportunity for mischief. To have a work destined to make its way in the world dismissed in full view of some two million newspaper readers as unworthy of their attention is a greater shock than if you could bring yourself round to agree with your traducer (as it is a greater shock to have your brilliant rather than backward child fail to gain a scholarship). Coleridge never lost an opportunity of reasoning against 'the head-dimming, heart-damping principle of judging a work by its defects, not its beauties. Every work must have the former—we know it *a priori*—but every work has not the latter, and he, therefore, who discovers them, tells you something that you could not with certainty, or even with probability, have anticipated.'

The popular belief in the infallibility of doctors and judges extends also to printed opinion, as though even casual labourers in that most unskilled of all trades known as reviewing must be immune from the usual percentage of plausible humbugs successfully simulating the outward forms and gestures of professional procedure everywhere else. The tricks have been well noted by Carlyle. The reviewer perches himself on the shoulder of his author and from there looks down upon him as though by natural superiority of stature. He professes with an air of knowingness and condescending mockery that this and that is beyond his comprehension, cunningly asking his readers if *they* comprehend. With a sudden access of emotion (lest he be thought uniformly malicious) he implores the author to forego his transcendental crotchets and write only thus, and *he* will admire him. He allows him genius—but not logic, and doubts if the writer himself really knows what his book is about. The Edinburgh carter, asked whether his horse could draw inferences, replied: 'Yes—anything in reason,' but a man of letters is evidently devoid of a faculty possessed even by a horse. In this way does the reviewer triumph over the author. 'But,' says Carlyle, 'it is the triumph of a fool. In this way, too, does he recommend himself to certain readers, but it is the recommendation of a parasite and of no true servant.' Or else, angered by his gush over your previous book, he revenges

'The Triumph of a Fool'

himself by undue sobriety over its successor. If, however, you give him time to get over his spleen, he eventually comes round to a new bout of critical regard, and the merits or demerits of your book have the least to do with it. This is the experience of every writer who knows what he wants to write and writes it in the only way literature can be written, as a consequence of your own, and not another's, vision: all advice to go back or turn a new leaf or, as Arnold Bennett urged, to write a new book *exactly* like the last—but different, notwithstanding.

The Dolorous Road

When on the dolorous road of letters I stop and sigh that the writer's, like the transgressor's, road is hard, a friend of mine replies impatiently that every life is hard—a bricklayer's no less than the poet's. And perhaps a work of art is in truth a transgression in that nothing, as Santayana insists, is ever truly possessed or recovered save under the form of eternity, which is also the form of art; and art so conceived is a premature peep into the future state. But for art, we would not notice, indeed never guess, how beautiful, with an unearthly beauty, stripped of habit and anxiety, is every day, every hour that passes by, of this our life on earth, too wonderful to conceive; unseen, unrealized, save by the saints and poets who have recorded the visage as an acquisition for all souls, this side the grave.

* * * * *

'Mr. Wordsworth,' we are told, 'was to propose to himself as his object to give the charm of novelty to things of every day, and to excite a feeling analogous to the supernatural, by awakening the mind's attention from the lethargy of custom, and directing it to the loveliness and the wonders of the world before us; an inexhaustible treasure, but for which, in consequence of the film of familiarity and selfish solicitude, we have eyes, yet see not, ears that hear not, and hearts that neither feel nor understand.' So wrote his friend and contemporary. 'The rapt one of the godlike forehead' Wordsworth calls him. And this brings me to that holy ground where poet and mystic unawares meet—the utterance of the ineffable. I call four independent witnesses, unconscious of one another's words, yet all alighting in that undiscovered country, wind-swept of day-dreams, day-dreams of our own making that St. Thomas Aquinas calls phantasms, and all alike partaking of that rare vision of reality when, clear of 'the confusion which sleep has shed upon our world,' we suddenly see, in an illumination one would almost say stereoscopic in focusing real things in the round, 'these simple and reasonable things' existing in their own right with an ecstatic, vibrant intensity of their own. 'The world is real, houses and trees, men and women, motor-buses and the moaning sea,' Hugh Kingsmill writes: 'But we have fallen asleep, and all these things, these simple and reasonable things, have been confused for us.'

The Stereoscopic Vision

Speaking of the powers of the mind to receive direct knowledge, not distorted in transmission through the senses or embellished by our egocentric association of ideas (which each of us privately mistakes for reality), St. Thomas Aquinas continues: 'But when the soul is separated from the body it understands no longer by turning to phantasms but by turning to simple intelligible objects.' And Tolstoy in effect tells us that Prince Andrew, having died and then for a day or two regained consciousness, could no longer understand the living, blindly following their own association of ideas and mistaking what was in fact a cloying web of phantasms of their own imagining for the 'simple intelligible objects,' 'these simple and reasonable things' his soul had already turned to beyond the mystery.

This naïve stereoscopic vision of reality (perhaps best defined as enamoured detachment from—yes: *from*—simple intelligible objects) is, of course, what Goethe meant also when, at a loss to make himself understood by writers so high-falutin over their aesthetic but quite unable to see, as he puts it, '*worauf es eigentlich ankommt*' (' what really is at stake'), he groped towards a definition of poetic literature as innocent love of real things concealing the Absolute (all but identical with Wordsworth's ' pleasure which there is in life itself' and Coleridge's ' feelings as fresh as if all had then sprung forth at the first creative fiat.') All else, said Goethe, being an attempt to pass off for literature what positively was *not* literature.

' Worauf es eigentlich ankommt'

To call a supernumerary witness, there is Proust who defines the poetic vision in the same sense as a spontaneous identification of a naïve sensation in the present with a similar sensation in the past—a sudden breath of unalloyed reality lifting one clean out of Time into the inutterably pure state of timeless being; the function of literature being to forge the ecstasy in the immutable chains of the analogy which recalls it, and so to shelter it from the hazards and erosion of Time. The analogy may be of little interest; the two objects interposed to release the sensation common to both may be more than mediocre; the style may be wretched; but so long as there has not been the release of this ecstasy of reality exuded by simple intelligible objects, there has been nothing.

* * * * *

Now why am I dwelling on all this? Because if you cannot recognize the stereoscopic vision in literature, or can discern no trace of it in my writing, you are not my ideal reader. Far be it from me to suggest that writing is an indulgent form of self-expression. It is a passion for communicating one's discoveries. The writer communicates: but always to the ideal reader. It is open to anyone to become one's ideal reader; but not open to a writer other than a journalist to write for any other reader. But my

My Ideal Reader

ideal reader—a being capable of tender sympathy deepened by humorous discernment—is not necessarily a highbrow. To identify this word with a criterion of taste and perception is to suppose that precisely there where pretentious obscurity is most secure from detection—in a fog of words—there are no fools or poltroons, as elsewhere. But that incoherence is the first refuge of a fake must not blind us to the special merits of implicit, as against explicit, poetry; and the novel, thanks to its honest prose and the daylight of recurring sanity of exposition and elucidation, must inevitably light up the twilight and the night of genuine implicitness, on pain of giving the impression of, let us say, *King Lear* (the greatest plays really being the most perfectly constructed novels) written—as Kingsmill has described the difference—not by Shakespeare but by King Lear.

Other things being equal, one might reasonably prefer the obscurity even of an imbecile implicit statement like 'In Woman we go back to the Father, but like the witnesses of the Transfiguration, blind and unconscious,' which throws off an obscure poetic gleam of nothing in particular coloured by the authorship of D. H. Lawrence, to a plain explicit statement, like: 'Nat had a cat but no rat'; though there are equally passionate admirers of the Gertrude Stein school who would seem to favour the latter crystal-clear method which, they claim, throws off an association even more obscure than the former.

Long Ears

At the other extreme, when Mozart's father advised him to write for the popular ear, Mozart said that he wrote for every kind of ear except long ones. The analphabetic who does not like books qualifies his ignorance by saying: 'I like a *good* book,' thus arrogating to himself the privilege of judgment, to make up for the lack of knowledge upon which to base it. The maxim 'Until you understand a writer's ignorance, presume yourself ignorant of his understanding,' is a counsel of perfection from the father of modern criticism. It is not in human nature to give credit to the writer for more wisdom and beauty than we ourselves have been able to receive. The reading public is not divided into highbrows and lowbrows but into innumerable individuals none of whom doubts the sufficiency of his own intelligence. It follows that it is not indifference to patient merit but unmerited faith in one's own competence to detect the unworthy which totals up to the oppressor's wrong, the proud man's contumely, that retard appreciation of original work. Recognition of your having broken new ground must wait upon others rolling up the open path—as like as not to tell you that there is nothing in it. And there is nothing for it but to hack away at the tunnel of art for the joy of light it will bring you and your reader tapping hopefully at the other end.

Audience of Genius

Assuming you are a writer of consummate genius, you will have cause to complain that your purest emanations fall on deaf ears. But you have no cause to complain. For if your genius did not fall on deaf ears, if your transcendental crotchets were immediately accessible, your subtlest emotions readily shared, your judgments seen a mile off to be just, it would only mean that your contemporaries were an audience of consummate genius from which your own did not stand out by an inch, and that the genius they were applauding was not yours but their own, and their recognition of you was in fact a recognition that you were of the common herd.

* * * * *

'But do you claim,' you might justifiably ask, 'to see everything under the aspect of eternity?' Since Time seen under the aspect of eternity is the very essence of literature —*ideally*, yes—everything. Time seen under the aspect of Time is called journalism. 'Then,' you say, 'you must be terribly earnest, and I don't like earnestness.' I am serious, but not earnest; humour, I need hardly say, being the most serious quality in literature. Earnestness is merely the exaggerated tribute we pay to Time. Newspaper articles pandering to their readers' passing moods are very earnest. But humour is clairvoyance in the service of this life. It is pure perception. It is independent of one's likes and dislikes; independent of self-pity; independent of one's interests. Linked with its counterpart, pathos, humour is as stereoscopic in its double focus of life as the mystic vision of 'simple intelligible objects,' and it has the same approach of enamoured detachment: nothing cloying or possessive here. For humour is affection unsullied either by personal associations or the greed of reciprocity: pure happiness. 'The humorous writer,' says Thackeray, 'professes to awaken and direct your love, your pity, your kindness—your scorn for untruth, pretension, imposture—your tenderness for the weak, the poor, the oppressed, the unhappy.' Pure disinterestedness. When all is said, purity of insight into the humorous tragedy of life is perhaps the highest criterion of art. It is an adolescent trait of criticism to identify solemnity with seriousness. To say, in fact, that the groans of the blind mole burrowing up towards the light are the most profound concern of literature is not to be aware that such profundity is but the measure of the distance yet to be traversed from the burrow to the surface of the earth. The lark is not inferior to the mole, only more gifted to soar into the light, and, out-distancing the creature of dark earth, he is nearer the heart of the mystery. What is light? What is serious? Purity of feeling being the only poetic criterion, it does not matter whether the poet touches the divine penumbra enveloping all life in contemplating a daisy or a Glasgow slum. Mozart is not inferior to Beethoven. It is no less serious to sing the

The Serious v. The Earnest

Light and Light

praises of the Lord than to groan aloud that God might bestir himself and put the world to rights. Each attitude presupposes a world perfect in completion, whole in perfection.

Critics feel uneasy when a writer is not solemn. Who is he laughing *at*? who *with*? Warily they trot out the stupid word 'satire,' or the silliest word of all 'sophistication,' which, if it means anything at all (and in French it significantly means falsification), can only mean a simulation of the mere contours of brilliance, necessitating the most vapid trading on false pretences. Make-belief it is, tacitly accepted as a socially-intellectual tradition by poltroons of both sexes, nervous lest by not joining loyally in the conspiracy of would-be smart if pointless cynicism they might disqualify

X-Ray v. Red Tooth

themselves from being thought intellectually bright if they are socially smart; or, worse still, from being thought smart if they are bright; or, more maddening of all, from being thought both smart *and* bright if they are neither. This eager readiness to class any kind of humour above the standard piece of slipping over a banana skin as 'satire' is prompted more by cowardice than natural stupidity. Laughter being commonly regarded as a cruel chase of unidentified victims in hatred and malice (an occupation, as Proust would say, 'd'ailleurs peu probable'), it is safer to join in full cry with that biting, writing hound than to run with the bitten hare. The much-vaunted distinction between laughing with and laughing at your characters has always seemed to me unreal, because if you are laughing *with* your characters you must be laughing with them *at* some other characters. But the reader, who hopes the author is laughing with him at his own characters, promptly labels them as creatures beneath his notice. A humorous writer is, next to God, the last creator in the world to despise his creatures. In the spirit of charity commended in the harlot and the publican he loves them, not because they are publicans and harlots, but because *he* is everything that Christ discerned as commendable in these professions, unjustly maligned (as is in fact their brother expert in human nature, the writer) as sinister and callous opportunists. It was Wagner who spoke of knowledge through compassion (' durch Mitleid wissend '). ' Durch Humor liebend' is true of the feelings entertained by the humorous writer for the very characters whom, the reader imagines, he is flaying alive. The malice traditionally attributed to laughter, as though the writer were a mad dog prowling about wondering whom he might bite, arises from the misconception that savage wit is the more penetrating because the more vicious ; whereas the X-ray, not the red tooth, is the real measure of incisive illumination. An insight like Chehov's, for example, penetrates to a level immeasurably deeper than the superficial differences of men and race, to a bed-rock of common humanity where *all* human beings, as human beings, are frail, irresponsible, weak. Against this, their success or failure is shown to be irrelevant. ' Anyone,' he notes, 'who advises you to write only of the strong, successful and interesting means himself.' Whether the heroes of Stalingrad are, or are not, a different breed from Chehov's characters, certainly as normal, natural and intelligent as any of his readers, is essentially beside the point. Seen through that powerful, searching lens, that unique vision of compassionate humour, a Stalin or a Churchill might emerge as but another Uncle Vanya. His very humour is to portray the kind of people who, though quick to spot others, could never see that they were Chehov characters. And those of us tempted at best to dismiss them with ' There but for the grace of God——' merely confuse Divine Grace with their own blindness rather than embrace self-criticism in the light of the most searching of Shaw's sayings :

Compassionate Humour

' How do you know that you are not a fool ? '

* * * * *

'But what,' you ask, 'of plot?' Certainly! 'Character-drawing?' Of course! 'Local colour? conflict? situation? dénouement?' Oh, yes! 'Manners?' Thank you! 'Suffering?' M'm! 'They are surely necessary?' And how! Plot is as old as Homer, and as respectable. It is a vehicle; it is inestimable for carrying what it contains. But—and that accounts for the success of so much meretricious fiction—it runs as well, and better, empty. Henry James is a perfect wizard at beating about the bush of conjecture, getting his Nosey Parkers to work you up into a froth of suspense—over anything—were it only mislaying his bedroom slippers—and then, lest you should think he has been trifling with you and be angry with him for having led you up the garden path, he takes you to an outhouse at the back and—look!—shows you, sheepishly, a corpse. Thank you very much. The spiritually backward fill their being, deflated by habit, with the suspense of hope and fear. They kill time rather than savour its beauty, rare though it be. All appurtenances for keying up your interest: the clash of personalities, the solution of problems, the extrication of characters from invidious situations: these are all crossword puzzles trotted out to hide the absence of poetry in the writer and the absence of any need of it in the reader. You may have them, too—the more the merrier—as secondary themes arising out of the poetry of life; but they are auxiliary services employed in furthering, carrying, dressing, feeding, managing 'the pleasure which there is in life itself,' the poetry of life exuded by 'simple intelligible objects,' 'these simple, reasonable things...houses and trees, men and women, motor-buses and the moaning sea.' If there has not been that positive accretion, that minimum residuum, the whole bag of tricks is a cheat and a swindle—a much-ado-about-nothing. This has always been my credo, and my quarrel has not been with windmills but with the stereo-blind... the progression of a cumulative understanding.

Suspense

William Gerhardie
19 Rossetti House
Hallam Street
London W.1